HEADLINE SERIES

Nos. 328/329   FOREIGN POLICY

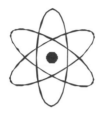

Seven minutes to midnight:
nuclear weapons after 9/11

Cover Design: Agnieshka Burke $14.99
Cover Photo: Doomsday Clock/Associated Press/AP
The symbolic clock, kept by the Bulletin of the Atomic Scientists, *had been set at 11:51 p.m. since 1998. It was moved to 11:53 p.m. on February 27, 2002.*

Author

RONALD J. BEE *is director of the Charles Hostler Institute on World Affairs at San Diego State University. Since November 2003, he has cochaired the military-to-military series, Arms Control and Regional Security Improvement in the Middle East. Bee has taught courses in national security policy, the conduct of American foreign relations, and WMD proliferation at the USDA Graduate School, San Diego State University, and the University of San Diego. He comments frequently for San Diego television and radio stations.*

The author dedicates this Headline Series
in memory of Ruth Adams and to Sandie and Chris Bee.

The Foreign Policy Association

The Foreign Policy Association is a private, nonprofit, nonpartisan educational organization. Its purpose is to stimulate wider interest and more effective participation in, and greater understanding of, world affairs among American citizens. Among its activities is the continuous publication, dating from 1935, of the HEADLINE SERIES. The author is responsible for factual accuracy and for the views expressed. FPA itself takes no position on issues of U.S. foreign policy.

HEADLINE SERIES (ISSN 0017-8780) is published occasionally by the Foreign Policy Association, Inc., 470 Park Avenue So., New York, NY 10016. Chairman, Gonzalo de Las Heras; President, Noel V. Lateef; Editor in Chief, Karen M. Rohan; Managing Editor, Ann R. Monjo; Art and Production Editor, Agnieshka Burke; Associate Editor, Nicholas Y. Barratt. Subscription rates, $30.00 for 4 issues. Single copy price $8.99; double issue $14.99; special issue $12.99. Discount 15% on 10 to 99 copies; 20% on 100 to 499; 25% on 500 and over. Payment must accompany all orders. (See order form on the last page for domestic S&H fees.) For foreign subscriptions please add $9.00 for shipping and handling. Second-class postage paid at New York, NY, and additional mailing offices. POSTMASTER: Send address changes to HEADLINE SERIES, Foreign Policy Association, 470 Park Avenue So., New York, NY 10016. Copyright 2006 by Foreign Policy Association, Inc. Design by Agnieshka Burke. Printed at Signature Press, Amherst Junction, Wisconsin. Published Spring 2006.

Library of Congress Control Number: 2006925160
ISBN: 0-87124-218-4

Introduction

IN 1947, THE *BULLETIN OF THE ATOMIC SCIENTISTS,* a magazine founded by nuclear scientists based in Chicago who had worked on the first atomic bomb, created a Doomsday Clock to signal, in their view, how close the world had come to nuclear catastrophe. That year the clock stood at seven minutes to midnight. The cold war had begun, along with a superpower struggle that prompted a more than half-century-long nuclear arms race, more countries seeking and acquiring nuclear weapons, and a parallel struggle to limit or reduce if not abolish them. By 1947, the United States held an atomic monopoly, but the Soviet Union would soon erase that, in 1949. The cold-war nuclear crises of Korea, Quemoy and Matsu, Suez, Berlin, and above all, Cuba, still lay ahead. Nonetheless, those who knew their destructive power firsthand worried about how these fearful weapons that had played a role in ending World War II at Hiroshima and Nagasaki might in the next war truly cause "the war to end all wars" by obliterating civilization as it was known.

In 2006, the *Bulletin of the Atomic Scientists* still publishes and its editors still set the Doomsday Clock, whose minute hand has, over time, moved closer to or further away from midnight depending on their assessment of the current nuclear danger. For 2006, as in 1947, the clock stands at seven minutes to midnight.

Then, as now, many questions about the future of nuclear weapons abound, about whether and how they might get used in anger, by design or by accident. While the cold-war rivalry and its arms race has thankfully ridden into the sunset, all the litter left along the way has yet to be cleaned up, and new nuclear threats now confront us in both national and transnational forms. And, perhaps most important, the Doomsday Clock did not in 1947 nor does it now indicate that nuclear doomsday remains inevitable, somehow like the passage of time. The sky is not falling; the world is not doomed to this fate. Rather the clock then and now serves as a warning to all to get moving on answering these important questions and rationally acting upon conclusions while there is still time.

In his acceptance speech for the 2005 Nobel Peace Prize, Dr. Mohamed ElBaradei said as much: "We are in a race against time," the Egyptian-born director general of the International Atomic Energy Agency (IAEA) argued. His

4

Nobel prize-winner Dr. Leon M. Lederman speaking on the occasion of the symbolic Doomsday Clock setting being moved two minutes closer to midnight on February 27, 2002, due to increased security threats. It was the 17th time the clock has been reset since it debuted in 1947.

Vienna-based organization serves as an international nuclear watchdog that since 1957 has aimed to prevent the spread of nuclear weapons to additional countries. This time, however, he warned of a new race, one that requires urgent efforts to keep nuclear weapons away from terrorists.

The September 11, 2001, Al Qaeda attacks on the World Trade Center, the Pentagon, and the flight over Pennsylvania heading toward the White House have served as a defining moment and organizing principle for the George W. Bush Administration. Those attacks made leaders worry about ter-

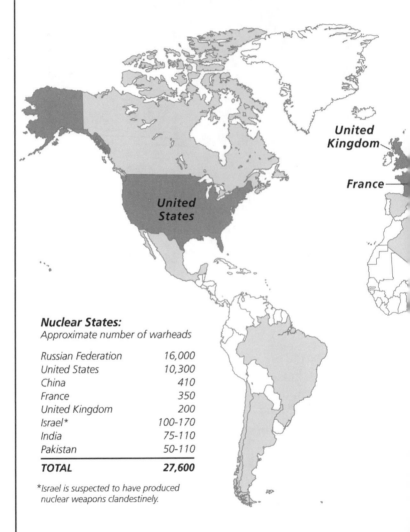

Nuclear Weapons Nations in 2006

United Kingdom

France

United States

Nuclear States:
Approximate number of warheads

Russian Federation	16,000
United States	10,300
China	410
France	350
United Kingdom	200
Israel*	100-170
India	75-110
Pakistan	50-110
TOTAL	**27,600**

*Israel is suspected to have produced nuclear weapons clandestinely.

Source: Carnegie Endowment for International Peace

NPT Nuclear Weapon States
Non-NPT Nuclear Weapon States
Suspected Clandestine Programs
Suspected Nuclear Weapon State
Abstaining countries

Russia

Pakistan

ael   Iran   China   North
                                    Korea

India

Abstaining Countries:

Algeria, Argentina, Australia, Austria, Belgium, Brazil, Bulgaria, Canada, Chile, Egypt, Finland, Germany, Hungary, Indonesia, Italy, Japan, Mexico, Netherlands, Norway, Poland, Romania, Republic of Korea, Slovakia, South Africa, Spain, Sweden, Switzerland, Taiwan, Turkey, Ukraine.

rorists, who use fear as their political currency, employing the ultimate weapons of fear—nuclear weapons—to make the next American "ground zero" a radioactive one. Because these weapons can kill hundreds of thousands within the blink of an eye, the United States wants to prevent them from falling into the wrong country's grasp, or worse, into the hands of terrorists.

In his diary on the night of 9/11, the President wrote, "The Pearl Harbor of the 21st century took place today." But September 11 went further than just mirroring the sneak attack on December 7, 1941, that required another American President to go to war. The 9/11 attacks also spoke to the atomic bombing of Hiroshima, Japan, on August 6, 1945. After September 11, many journalists used the phrase "ground zero" to describe the rubble and gaping hole in lower Manhattan—the same language used in 1945 to describe the point of explosion for the Hiroshima blast. Imagine if New York's ground zero had suffered the explosion of a nuclear device like the one dropped on Hiroshima.

That prospect evidently faced the President and New York City exactly one month to the day after 9/11. According to Graham Allison, Harvard professor, former government official and author of the book *Nuclear Terrorism: The Ultimate Preventable Catastrophe*, Central Intelligence Agency (CIA) director George J. Tenet told the President in his October 11, 2001, daily intelligence briefing that Al Qaeda terrorists had evidently stolen a 10-kiloton nuclear bomb from the Russians, smuggled it into the United States, and brought it to New York City. Afraid that terrorists might also have transported one to Washington, D.C., President Bush ordered Vice President Dick Cheney to leave town for an indefinite period to guarantee succession of government in case of attack. Bush then ordered a Nuclear Emergency Support Team (NEST) to New York City to look for the weapon. To avoid panic, the team of scientists and engineers did not inform anyone, including Mayor Rudolph Giuliani.

While the NEST team found nothing, and no nuclear weapon detonated, the incident served as a wake-up call for the President. Evidence continued to mount about Al Qaeda's interest in nuclear weapons, as well as how the unfriendly states of Iraq, Iran and North Korea were continuing to develop them in defiance of the United Nations and the Nuclear Non-Proliferation Treaty (NPT), an accord on the books since 1970. All three nations had signed the NPT, which forbids building nuclear weapons, all three had not-so-secret nuclear programs, and all three had denied UN IAEA inspectors access to investigate suspicious activities. And all three could sell or give their nuclear wares to terrorists.

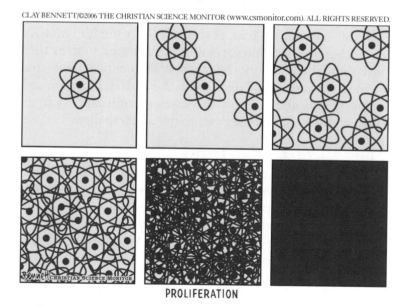

PROLIFERATION

Nuclear weapons remain the most deadly and destructive weapons possessed by humankind. That, above all, has not changed since 9/11. On Halloween 1961, the Soviets tested the largest nuclear weapon ever detonated, a 58-megaton blast, nearly 4,000 times more powerful than the Hiroshima bomb.

Before nuclear weapons, trinitrotoluene, commonly known as TNT, represented the most powerful known explosive. When nuclear weapons appeared, their explosive power became quantified in kilotons (thousands of tons) or megatons (millions of tons) of TNT.

While the Soviet explosion represented the largest nuclear test ever conducted, it also signaled that nuclear weapons represent the granddaddy of the so-called family of weapons of mass destruction (WMD). Chemical and biological weapons represent the two other grisly and deadly forms of WMD. While a few deaths from anthrax letters sent in the mail can cause much fear, as they did after the 9/11 attacks, and a chemical weapon can kill those exposed to it, as they have throughout history, the prospect of a nearly 60-megaton weapon obliterating a large city with its blast, firestorm and lingering radioactivity puts this category of weaponry in an entirely different class of destruction and lethality.

Nexus of Nukes and Terrorism

The end of the cold war gave way to a set of different threats that now point directly to a nexus of nuclear weapons and terrorism. What should the United States believe, let alone do, about nuclear weapons post-9/11?

In a 2005 speech to the Philadelphia World Affairs Council, U.S. Secretary of Defense Donald H. Rumsfeld argued that Americans must first recognize the new threats and the changing face of war since 9/11. Regarding the 9/11 attacks,

and terrorist goals and tactics, Rumsfeld asserted, "Their goal, very simply, is to cripple the United States, to try to intimidate the civilized world, and to inspire and cultivate a new wave of fanatics….We confront an enemy unburdened by bureaucracy or regulation—or any legal, moral or structural constraints….They combine medieval views with modern tools and technology." Terrorists need many things, he said, including ideological support to recruit new terrorists, leadership, command structures, communications networks, safe harbors, financial support and access to targets in free nations. And they need weapons, Rumsfeld emphasized, "potentially to include chemical, biological, or nuclear." Terrorists, he concluded, "are unlikely to ever give up; and symbolized by beheadings, they seek to impose a dark, joyless vision upon the future of our world."

11

Using Atoms for Peace or for Weapons Development

MOST NUCLEAR WEAPONS today still rely on tapping the enormous explosive potential found within the nucleus of highly enriched uranium 235 (used in the Hiroshima bomb) or plutonium 239 (used in the Nagasaki bomb). The "dual-use" nature of nuclear materials makes them usable for either peaceful production of energy in reactors or for the building of explosive devices.

To create energy, most nuclear reactors need U235 to sustain a controlled chain reaction to produce electrical power. U235, if used in the right quantity, quality and weapons design, can also serve as a nuclear explosive. Experiments conducted during World War II showed that U235 atoms proved less stable and therefore more likely to break apart or "fission" when bombarded with neutrons and in large enough quantities to produce a sustainable chain reaction. When fission occurs, enormous amounts of energy get released.

Thankfully, U235 remains a rare material. In nature, 99.3 percent of all uranium exists as U238 (92 protons and 146 neutrons); only 0.7 percent exists as U235 (92 protons and 143 neutrons). U235 is always found mixed together with U238. To obtain U235, technicians use separation techniques based on the slight weight difference between U235 and

U238 atoms. These separation processes, called "enrichment," create the highly enriched uranium for either peaceful use in certain reactor types or for use in military weapons. Qualified inspectors from the IAEA can tell the difference, if they can get permission to inspect all nuclear facilities and activities. Getting that permission remains all-important, and deciding how to enforce international law against noncompliant states remains controversial.

All "fission reactors" produce plutonium PU239, a nuclear fissile material often preferred in weapon designs, as nuclear weapons need less plutonium than uranium to produce the same explosive effect (also known as "yield"). Reasonably pure plutonium, however, can only come from withdrawing the uranium fuel after a short period (2–6 months) from the reactor core. "Reprocessing" of spent reactor fuel describes a process whereby U235 and PU239 get separated from the other "fission byproducts" by chemical means. The uranium can get recycled back into reactor fuel, or diverted for use in nuclear weapons. Plutonium can be stored, sold or diverted for use in nuclear weapons. When ElBaradei of the IAEA says a new framework for using nuclear technology must be found, he means controlling the nuclear fuel cycle in such a way as to prevent U235 and PU239 misuse for the creation of nuclear weapons. ∎

Some still remain unconvinced and believe the overblown "threat of terrorism" has simply replaced the old cold-war "threat of communism." Senator Robert C. Byrd (D-W.Va.) contended that the Bush Administration simply exaggerated intelligence reports of Iraq's WMD and links to Al Qaeda to justify war. Senator Byrd believed that President Bush had used the WMD card as "weapons of mass deception" to invoke public fear and build support for the invasion of Iraq in March 2003.

Others like former Senator Sam Nunn (D-Ga.) assert that the United States should worry about terrorists getting nuclear materials and therefore should stop the transfer at its most likely sources. In 1991, after the Soviet Union had dissolved, Senators Nunn and Richard Lugar (R-Ind.) co-sponsored the Soviet Nuclear Threat Reduction Act (also known as the Nunn-Lugar act) that became central to U.S. efforts to denuclearize the former Soviet Union. This law authorized helping the Russians destroy nuclear weapons, transport, store, disable and safeguard them, and establish verifiable safeguards against nuclear materials proliferation. As of 2005, according to Nunn, "we and the Russians ... [had] completed between 25 percent and 50 percent of the job" and the program "recently gained renewed support on Capitol Hill and in the White House."

Senator Nunn, who now leads a nonprofit group called the Nuclear Threat Initiative (NTI), on March 9, 2005, asserted, "We are in a race between cooperation and catastrophe, and the threat is outrunning our response." The senator has pointed out two worrisome nuclear terrorism scenarios: a terrorist attack with a nuclear weapon or a terrorist attack with a "dirty bomb" (a conventional explosive incorporating radioactive material). Making his point, in 2003 the United States discovered that the father of the Pakistani nuclear

Feb. 5, 2004: Rally in honor of Pakistan's Abdul Qadeer Khan,
father of the "Islamic Bomb," who was pardoned by
President Gen. Pervez Musharraf for providing technology to
Iran, Libya and North Korea.

bomb, Abdul Qadeer Khan, had established a private business network that allegedly sold know-how, technology and
fissile materials to Libya, Iran and North Korea (the Democratic People's Republic of Korea, or DPKR). If Khan could
sell to states with cash, why couldn't he or other nuclear
entrepreneurs sell to terrorists with cash?

Still others wonder if the linchpin for preventing the
spread of nuclear weapons, the NPT, has simply lost its lus-
ter and the UN its credibility because at least three signatories—Iraq, North Korea and Iran—have defied the treaty
by openly developing nuclear weapons programs. Shouldn't
that crucial cold-war treaty be reformed or revised to deal
with post-cold-war realities? Dr. ElBaradei, who heads the

IAEA, the UN's NPT watchdog, certainly thinks the NPT needs reform. Before the five-year NPT review conference in May 2005 began, he argued, "...We need a new framework for using nuclear technology for the 21st century."

That month-long 2005 NPT Review Conference, however, ended in discord, with strong disagreements over priorities for curbing nuclear weapons proliferation. The 188 current NPT signatories reviewed prospective measures and could not agree on how to proceed. The United States focused on the threats of Iran and North Korea while thwarting any document that referred to the U.S. 1995 and 2000 pledges

Developed by the laboratories headed by Indian-born, German-educated A.Q. Khan, the Ghauri missile is shown in a successful launching test in April 1998. Shortly thereafter, Pakistan announced its ability to equip the Ghauri with nuclear warheads.

to disarm. Iran insisted its program only exists for producing energy while blocking anything that referred to it as a proliferation threat and NPT violator. Egypt joined the fray and proposed, as it has since the mid-1970s, that the conference address Israel's nuclear status and declare the Middle East a "nuclear-weapons-free zone." North Korea had withdrawn from the NPT in 2003. Israel, India and Pakistan, however, have not signed the NPT, and have suffered no extensive international consequences for "going nuclear."

While some delegates to the NPT review conference blamed Washington and Tehran (Iran's capital) for lack of progress, one European diplomat observed that in such a post-cold-war, post-September 11 world, the NPT's contract of "exchanging disarmament against nonproliferation is a false equation. We must seize the reality that the main challenge today is monitoring the peaceful use of nuclear energy" as such use can and does veil nuclear weapons programs. Moreover, nations must start dealing with "nonstate actors," the buzzword for terrorists without any recognized uniform or flag that now seek to acquire WMD for their own political purposes.

As new terrorist threats, potential nuclear terrorism, problematic NPT signatories and problematic NPT nonsignatories suggest, little if anything remains "simple" when it comes to assessing the threats that nuclear weapons pose and the best policies to deal with them. While the end of the cold war helped reduce the predominant nuclear arsenals in the United States and Russia, some 25,000–30,000 nuclear weapons remain in those two and in at least seven other national arsenals of Britain, France, China, India, Pakistan, Israel and North Korea. And other regional cold wars now loom.

In May 1998, both India and Pakistan openly tested nuclear weapons and declared their nuclear status. The United

STRATEGIC NUCLEAR ARMS CONTROL AGREEMENTS

	SALT I	SALT II	START I	START II	START III	SORT*
Deployed Warhead Limit	Limited Missiles, Not Warheads	Limited Missiles and Bombers, Not Warheads	6,000	3,000–3,500	2,000–2,500	1,700–2,200
Deployed Delivery Vehicle Limit	U.S.: 1,710 ICBMs & SLBMs; USSR: 2,347 ICBMs & SLBMs	2,250	1,600	Not Applicable	Not Applicable	Not Applicable
Status	Expired	Never Entered Into Force	In Force	Never Entered Into Force	Never Negotiated	Signed, Awaits Ratification
Date Signed	May 26, 1972	June 18, 1979	July 31, 1991	Jan. 3, 1993	Not Applicable	May 24, 2002
Date Entered Into Force	Oct. 3, 1972	Not Applicable	Dec. 5, 1994	Not Applicable	Not Applicable	?
Implementation Deadline	Not Applicable	Dec. 31, 1981	Dec. 5, 2001	Dec. 31, 2007	Dec. 31, 2007	Dec. 31, 2012
Expiration Date	Oct. 3, 1977	Dec. 31, 1985	Dec. 5, 2009	Dec. 5, 2009	Not Applicable	Dec. 31, 2012

*Strategic Offensive Reductions Treaty

SOURCE: ARMS CONTROL ASSOCIATION

States imposed sanctions, but within six months started lifting them and has since relaxed them to the point of embarking on a strategic relationship with India (during the Clinton Administration) and relying on Pakistan as a key ally in the war against terrorism (during the Bush Administration). Nonproliferation experts and former government officials Kurt Campbell and Robert Einhorn have concluded, "Would-be proliferators no doubt took notice of the mild international consequences for breaching the nuclear ramparts."

In October 2002, one such nuclear aspirant, North Korea, admitted to a secret uranium enrichment program, thus violating its earlier 1994 Agreed Framework that prohibited any nuclear weapons activities. North Korea resumed all activities, expelled all UN inspectors, and withdrew from the NPT. In February 2005, North Korea publicly declared its own nuclear capability, signaling that it might soon test a weapon to prove it. Six-party negotiations involving China, Japan, Russia, North Korea, South Korea and the United States got under way in August 2003 with their aim of thwarting the North Korean nuclear weapons program.

After three rounds of six-party talks, the North Koreans stopped attending. Instead, in May 2005, they chose to test-launch a ballistic missile into the Sea of Japan, making the Japanese more nervous about a day when North Korea could marry a nuclear warhead with a ballistic missile to reach their island nation. In late April, Vice Admiral Lowell Jacoby, head of the Defense Intelligence Agency, did not help those jitters when at a Senate hearing he indicated that North Korea has the capacity to arm a missile with a nuclear device. At some point, the Japanese and South Koreans may reconsider whether to build their own nuclear arsenals in response (for now, both countries rely on the United States for deterrence through bilateral defense alliances). At a minimum, the North Korean missile tests over Japan have forced the Japanese to think about building a missile defense system.

The South Koreans and the Chinese, worried about the consequences of a war on the Korean peninsula, their immediate neighborhood, hesitated to take the issue to the UN Security Council, which could recommend economic sanctions against the DPRK. Both countries provide aid and trade to North Korea. Pyongyang, the North Korean capital, has repeatedly warned that any sanctions levied against it would amount to a declaration of war. Instead, the United States suggested, as it did during the 1962 Cuban missile crisis, a "quarantine" that can permit a peaceful resolution of the crisis. North Korea has said it considers any "blockade" or "economic sanctions" as an act of war. But North Korea, unlike Cuba, has Communist China with over a billion people on its northern border, and some one million troops deployed along the DMZ (demilitarized zone) between North and South Korea. The United States, with 29,500 troops on the DMZ, can ill afford another war, one that could soon go nuclear, and one that would sap attention away from the goal of 130,000 U.S. troops supporting a fledgling Iraqi democracy. Under back-channel encouragement from the Chinese and the Americans, the North Koreans agreed to return to the negotiating table.

That led to a fourth and fifth round of six-party talks and to a "joint statement" on September 19, 2005, where a compromise between the United States and North Korea created the basis for a deal. The North Koreans would abandon their nuclear activities and rejoin the NPT in exchange for the United States agreeing not to invade North Korea and energy assistance from South Korea. The next talks would have to identify concrete measures that could lead to the fulfillment of the joint statement. In March 2006, however,

Beijing, July 26, 2005: Chinese Foreign Minister Li Zhaoxing (center) poses with negotiators for the fourth round of six-party talks on North Korea's nuclear program.

in response to planned U.S.-South Korean military exercises, North Korea vowed to strengthen its "peaceful nuclear activities," leading some to believe the North Korean nuclear issue is still a threat.

In the Middle East, Iran may have also learned from the India and Pakistan example, let alone North Korea's nuclear postures that serve to preserve its authoritarian regime, deter the United States, and fish for benefits through negotiation. In 2002, Iranian dissidents revealed that Iran had secretly built two sensitive nuclear facilities in defiance of IAEA regulations and inspectors. Subsequent IAEA investigations led its director general to report on November 11, 2003: "Iran has lied systematically about its nuclear programs for 18 years, seeking to hide the development of key technologies needed to make fissile material for nuclear weapons." Iran entered into European Union (EU-3) negotiations with Britain, France and Germany which, in exchange for freezing and eventually ending Iran's nuclear weapons activities, seek to offer political and economic concessions. By August of 2005, Iranian elections had brought the hard-line, anti-American Mahmoud Ahmadinejad to power as the president of the Islamic Republic of Iran, making prospects for any European nuclear deal with Iran far more difficult. Three rounds of EU-3 talks with Tehran failed to persuade Iran to stop its nuclear enrichment activities. Iran claims it will use nuclear energy to generate electricity but the United States suspects oil-rich Tehran remains intent on developing nuclear weapons. The EU now concurs. On March 1, 2006, the IAEA board of governors referred Iran to the UN Security Council for action. In the absence of a negotiated deal with Iran, some form of international economic sanctions, and ultimately military action, remain on the table as possible options. In the meantime, Iran must choose between international cooperation or conflict.

Israel, with its own "ambiguous" nuclear arsenal (Israel neither admits or denies having one), rests uneasy when Islamist Iran, which views Israel as its sworn enemy, speaks about its right to enrich uranium. (In October 2005, Iranian President Ahmadinejad publicly called for Israel to be "wiped off" the map.) Israel, and for that matter the United States, now hopeful with the passing of Yasir Arafat (longtime leader of the Palestine Liberation Organization) in 2004 that Israelis and Palestinians can achieve a final peace settlement, does not want a nuclear Iran inciting terrorism through

Hezbollah, Hamas and Islamic Jihad. And Hamas, having won a majority of seats in January 2006 in the Palestinian Parliament, must choose between governing or violence. As with Iran, many question marks about the future of the Israeli-Palestinian conflict remain.

Iraq, which shares an 800-mile border with Iran and fought a bloody war from 1980 to 1988 with that country, worries as its fledgling government struggles to take shape that an emboldened nuclear Iran might meddle in its internal affairs or fuel the ongoing insurgency. The United States, for its part, having fought two wars in Iraq, has deployed its forces and bet the farm on a self-governing Iraq to serve as a democratic beacon for the future of a peaceful Middle East.

Besides North Korea and Iran, terrorists also seek the power that nuclear weapons convey, the fear that they generate, and the bargaining power they can leverage. According to many reports, Al Qaeda has sought to find, build or buy WMD for over a decade. And especially in the case of suicidal terrorists, cold-war deterrence—nuclear or conventional—no longer works against those without a national address who plan to kill themselves along with their intended victims. For this reason, and with 9/11 constantly in mind, President Bush chose to adopt a strategy of pre-emption in a global war against terrorism, a strategy that also backed the invasions of Afghanistan and Iraq.

In September 2002, six months before Operation Iraqi Freedom, Dr. Condoleezza Rice, then national security adviser, now secretary of state, acknowledged that "there will always be some uncertainty" in determining how close Iraq may have gotten to obtaining a nuclear weapon, but added, "We don't want the smoking gun to be a mushroom cloud."

With all these scary developments and new nuclear threats, what hope or optimism can the world possibly summon up?

How can the world push back the minute hand on the clock? Human beings, despite a tendency to worry about doomsday in every era, have thus far found a way to avoid it. Some pure human luck may have played a role. Many of those who remember diving under their desks during the Cuban missile crisis, viewing "Burt the Turtle" civil defense films, building bomb shelters, and waiting for superpower nuclear obliteration to occur have taken deep breaths, and noted with measurable relief that the earth still revolves around the sun and it is still our home.

After almost going to nuclear war over Cuba, the United States concluded arms control treaties like the 1963 Hotline Agreement and Limited Test Ban Treaty (LTBT), as well as

CHAPPATTE Int'l Herald Tribune

the NPT that gained widespread international support. In the 1980s and 1990s, the United States made unilateral cuts in its theater nuclear forces (TNF), negotiated bilateral intermediate nuclear forces (INF) and Strategic Arms Reductions Talks (START I and II) agreements, and, along with Russia, made deep cuts in arsenals and nuclear budgets—not to mention dismantling and destroying tens of thousands of nuclear weapons. With the dissolution of the Soviet Union, Belarus, Ukraine and Kazakhstan chose to relinquish their Soviet-era nuclear weapons and adhere to the NPT. In 1992, France and China finally signed the NPT, and in 1995 all its signatories agreed to the NPT's indefinite extension. Under the 2001 Moscow Treaty, which was drawn up by Bush and Russian President Vladimir Putin, the United States plans by 2112 to destroy up to 80 percent of its cold-war arsenal. In recent years, countries like Argentina, Brazil, South Africa and Libya decided to abandon their nuclear ambitions. South Africa and Libya chose to destroy their nuclear programs to avoid the astronomical costs, political liabilities and military threats involved in building and maintaining a nuclear arsenal.

In 1963 President John F. Kennedy predicted that by the 1970s there would be 15 to 20 nuclear weapons states. More than 40 years later, the world has done much better than that prediction. Only nine nations possess nuclear weapons. As 9/11 painfully indicated, however, different nuclear threats now come from nuclear-aspiring states and from nonstate actors who seek to tap the fear these most fearful weapons generate to promote their own causes.

In a poignant post-Cuban-missile-crisis speech, "Toward a Strategy of Peace," President Kennedy invoked mankind once again to find a way to avoid the perils facing it: "Our problems are manmade; therefore they can be solved by man." Over 40 years later, there clearly exists another nuclear crossroads and Kennedy's words still ring true today as the world seeks to manage its nascent fears and address the new nuclear threats of the post-9/11 era.

1

Four Fearful Nuclear Races

THE WORLD'S EXPERIENCE with nuclear weapons since World War II can be described in terms of four separate yet overlapping races. The first, involving the United States, Britain, and Nazi Germany began during World War II and ended with the bombing of Hiroshima and Nagasaki. The second, between the United States and the Soviet Union, began at the end of World War II and resulted in the building of enormous nuclear arsenals by both superpowers and the creation of smaller stockpiles by Britain, France and China. The third race involved (and still involves) preventing the spread or "proliferation" of nuclear weapons to other nations and has seen some successes. Saddam Hussein's Iraq, while clearly having pursued nuclear weapons programs, reluctantly relinquished them after an Israeli raid, two U.S.-led invasions and UN disarmament measures. The third race has also seen some failures, with Israel, India, Pakistan and North Korea choosing to join the nuclear club. The near-term challenges involve North Korea's small but growing nuclear weapons capability and Iran's threshold nuclear weapons program. The long-term challenge involves adjusting the rules, including the NPT, to keep the nuclear club as small as possible. Race number four began in earnest after 9/11, and overlaps the third race by aiming to prevent the existing nuclear weapons, materials, and know-how of nuclear weapons states from falling into the hands of terrorists.

Fear has underscored all four races because nuclear weapons can kill thousands, even millions, of human beings. McGeorge Bundy, national security adviser to Presidents Kennedy and Lyndon B. Johnson, concluded that fear stood out as the key factor that had driven the proliferation of nuclear weapons since their invention: "When we review the record, looking at the motives for the decisions of major governments, we find that while motive is…frequently somewhat mixed, the dominant theme, beginning with Franklin Roosevelt in 1941, is fear—if we don't get it first, he [Hitler] may…[Roosevelt] got it so we must—Stalin in 1945; they are doing it, so must we—Britain and France; they have done it, and we will—Mao ….Less fearful motives do operate: we will win; we will catch up; we will be great; we will even, perhaps, be safe. But fear dominates."

The First Race—Against the Nazis

The Nazis had begun work in 1939 on a secret nuclear weapons project code-named the "Uranium Society" shortly after two German scientists (Otto Hahn and Fritz Strassman) had discovered uranium fission in Berlin. After Hitler invaded Poland in September 1939, Albert Einstein, the famous German physicist and émigré, wrote U.S. President Franklin D. Roosevelt (1933–45) and warned him about the German bomb project, urging him to support U.S. atomic research as a prudent countermeasure. Since at that time the United States still remained officially neutral in the war, Roosevelt committed only modest initial support for an advisory committee on uranium.

U.S. neutrality and any remaining vestige of isolationism died a violent death when the Japanese attacked Pearl Harbor on December 7, 1941. The United States declared war on Japan the following day. Germany declared war on the United States three days later, and all of a sudden, Roosevelt had to pay more attention to German nuclear research. Through secret authorizations, he gathered together in the United States American and European scientists who created the first "nuclear arms race" with Hitler's Germany. Above all, U.S. and British leaders wanted to build atomic bombs before the Nazis could develop and use them against Allied forces and cities. Under the code name "Manhattan Project," the United States and Britain successfully engineered, constructed and tested an atomic bomb in Alamogordo, New Mexico, on July 16, 1945. By this time, however, Germany had already surrendered. Japan had not.

The Allies had already witnessed a global conflict responsible for some 55 million dead from "more conventional" weapons. After the first atomic test, British Prime Minister Winston Churchill dubbed the achievement "a miracle of deliverance." With U.S. casualties mounting as the fight got closer to the Japanese homeland, U.S. President Harry S. Truman (1945–53) ordered the atomic bombing of Hiroshima on August 6, and Nagasaki on August 9, 1945. World War II ended a month later.

The damage caused by these two weapons dwarfed any previously known explosive. "Little Boy," the enriched uranium device used on Hiroshima, and "Fat Man," the plutonium device used on Nagasaki, each generated heat that reached an estimated 1,000,000°F at ground zero, the epicenters of the nuclear detonations. In Hiroshima, an estimated 78,000 Japanese died instantly or soon thereafter from the blast, from fires and from radiation. Another 37,000 inhabitants of Hiroshima simply disappeared. In Nagasaki,

"FAT MAN"

"LITTLE BOY"

caglecartoons.com

©2002 FLORIDA TODAY JEFF PARKER

WWW.CAGLECARTOONS.COM/JEFF PARKER

the bomb missed its target by a mile and a half, still killing at least 40,000 Japanese, and injuring another 25,000. The city burned for over 24 hours, and radioactive dust called "fallout" began killing more victims there and in Hiroshima. On August 10, President Truman ordered a halt to all atomic bombings, saying to his Secretary of Commerce Henry Wallace that he thought it too horrible to wipe out another 100,000 people.

Germany, as it turned out, did not make serious progress toward producing nuclear weapons. The Communist Soviet Union, while an ally of the United States and Britain against fascism, did not receive an invitation to participate in the Manhattan Project. Soviet spies, however, did inform Stalin of Allied plans and progress from almost the very beginning. Stalin knew about the Manhattan Project as early as March 1942, when he responded by starting a secret Soviet nuclear bomb project. U.S. Vice President Truman, however, did not learn about the Manhattan Project until after Roosevelt's death on April 12, 1945.

The Soviet project took on new urgency after the U.S. bombings of Hiroshima and Nagasaki. Despite having lost about a tenth of its population and 30 percent of its national wealth during World War II, the Soviet Union began an all-out effort to build a nuclear weapon. The fears driving the first nuclear race had already begun fueling a second nuclear competition.

The Second Race—Between the Superpowers

The fear caused by these first weapons did not only linger in the radioactive rubble of Hiroshima and Nagasaki. In August 1945, Soviet leader Joseph Stalin commanded his people's commissar for munitions: "Provide us with atomic weapons in the shortest possible time. You know that Hiroshima has shaken the whole world. The equilibrium has been destroyed. Provide the bomb—it will remove a great danger from us."

After World War II, trepidation about the strategic consequences of nuclear weapons ultimately doomed early UN efforts from 1946 to 1949 to put the military uses of nuclear energy under effective international control. Nuclear weapons, and the fact that the United States had them and the Soviet Union did not, fueled the capitalist vs. Communist cold-war ideological struggle that led directly to a second nuclear arms race.

In August 1949 the Soviets tested their first nuclear weapon in Semipalatinsk, Soviet Kazakhstan. By design, the Sovi-

U.S. and U.S.S.R./Russian Nuclear Stockpiles, 1945-2012*

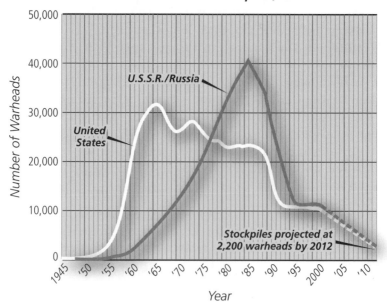

*According to the Treaty between U.S. and the Russian Federation on Strategic Offensive Reductions, May 24, 2002

ets tested a more or less copy of the U.S. Fat Man plutonium device used on Nagasaki, with an explosive yield of 20–22 kilotons. The RDS-1 (the Soviet acronym and code name for "First Lightning," or known to some as "Stalin's Rocket Engine"), dubbed "Joe 1" in the Western world, shocked many American officials who assumed the Soviets would need at least 20 years to build and test an atomic weapon.

After hearing the news, U.S. Ambassador George F. Kennan (1904–2005), the father of the U.S. Soviet containment policy, wrote, "There could be no greater protection for our own people against atomic attack than the deterrent effect of overwhelming retaliatory power in the hands of this country." U.S. strategists tapped the fear surrounding nuclear weapons along the lines Kennan suggested by threatening to use nuclear weapons to destroy anyone who attacked the United States or its allies. "Anyone" in this instance meant the Soviet Union, and everyone clearly witnessed a second nuclear arms race that initially focused on U.S. attempts to keep ahead and Soviet attempts to catch up.

The second race produced, at the height of the cold war, over 80,000 nuclear weapons deployed in a variety of sizes, with varying ranges, and on diverse delivery vehicles: nuclear "backpacks," short-, medium- and longer-range artillery, short-, medium- and intercontinental-range ballistic missiles (ICBMs), land-, sea- and air-based cruise missiles, nuclear submarines with ICBMs and nuclear bombers with nuclear gravity bombs. Both sides developed Multiple Independently Targeted Reentry Vehicles (MIRVs), small but powerful multiple warheads placed on a single ICBM that could drop many nuclear weapons onto different targets.

According to a Brookings Institution study, *Atomic Audit: The Costs and Consequences of U.S. Nuclear Weapons Since 1940*, the United States alone, from 1940 through 1996, spent an estimated $5.5 trillion (in constant 1996 dollars) on nuclear weapons and nuclear weapons-related programs, about 29 percent of all military spending during this period. Despite that exorbitant price tag, many cold warriors argue it proved worth it because that U.S. "investment" ultimately contributed to winning the cold war. The costs for the other nuclear nations that joined the nuclear club during the cold war are not known: the U.S.S.R. (first nuclear test in 1949), Britain (1952), France (1960) and China (1964).

The cold war demonstrated that nuclear weapons remain difficult to build, requiring huge investments in time, money, manpower and sophisticated technology. Nonetheless, the era also showed that if nations find nuclear weapons in their vital interest, they find a way to pay for them, whether or not all the human costs are known. That, too, has not changed since 9/11.

The Third Race—Against Nuclear Proliferation

After the jubilation that accompanied the end of World War II came a somber realization that humankind now possessed the means to destroy itself. President Truman reflected: "I realize the tragic significance of the atomic bomb....[It] is too dangerous to be loose in a lawless world.... We must constitute ourselves trustees of this new force—to prevent its misuse, and to turn it into the channels of service to mankind."

In August 1945, Truman authorized the release of the *Smyth Report*, a U.S. War Department document written by Princeton physicist Henry Smyth on the Manhattan Project. The report openly dealt with the problems faced and solutions needed for designing an atomic bomb. While the intent of publishing the document included signaling that the United States had nothing to hide, the Soviets mimeographed thousands of copies and distributed them to their scientists

34

working on their own bomb project. The third nuclear race had already begun.

Nonetheless, the United Nations, founded in 1945 at a time when the World War II rubble still smoldered, represented an international organizational hope for preventing future catastrophic wars. The UN Charter stated, "Twentieth-century man has become increasingly aware that world government is a necessary corrective to the dangers of aggressive nationalism, and that only cooperative international control can save man from his own destructive genius."

In November 1945, the United States, Britain and Canada proposed the establishment of a United Nations atomic energy commission with the purpose of "entirely eliminating the use of atomic energy for destructive purposes" and promoting its use for peaceful ends. Thus began a cold-war period when, according to Manhattan Project scientist and presidential adviser Herbert York, "building weapons while talking peace" got under way. While advocating international control of nuclear technology, both the United States and the Soviet Union accelerated nuclear arms development and, in the U.S. case, nuclear testing.

On June 14, 1946, Bernard M. Baruch, the American representative to the newly formed UN Atomic Energy Commission, presented a plan to establish a permanent international authority to control, inspect and license all nuclear reactors and materials to ensure their use for peaceful purposes only. The "Baruch Plan" proposed to destroy all U.S. nuclear weapons when the UN could agree on international controls, including enforcement provisions to punish violators. "If we fail," Baruch pleaded at the UN, "we have damned every man to be the slave of fear."

The Soviets, for their part, feared an American nuclear monopoly, rejected the Baruch Plan's verification measures and refused to permit UN inspections of U.S.S.R. territory. This represented the first time an active nuclear proliferator had refused UN inspections—a common theme that still resonates today among proliferating states.

The United States began a nuclear weapons testing program on the Bikini Atoll in the western Pacific Ocean only 16 days after proposing the Baruch Plan. The official Soviet newspaper *Pravda* charged that the United States "aimed not at restricting but perfecting atomic weapons," and that Americans really wanted just to maintain their nuclear monopoly as an instrument of international blackmail.

The first and some experts still think "best chance" for international control of nuclear weapons technology fell as an early victim of the cold-war superpower competition. By the 1950s, that competition had already produced large numbers of nuclear weapons. While their arsenals grew, the superpowers began worrying about the consequences of too many nations getting the bomb. An idea resurfaced during President Dwight D. Eisenhower's Administration (1953–61) about how international control of nuclear weapons proliferation might work if nuclear states helped nonnuclear states get access to the peaceful uses of nuclear energy. If nonnuclear states pledged to develop only civilian and nonmilitary uses, then nuclear states would in exchange make it easier for them to acquire nuclear technology and materials.

This "nuclear bargain," as it became called, sat at the center of Eisenhower's December 1953 "Atoms for Peace" plan proposed to the UN General Assembly, to "shake off the inertia imposed by fear." A product of Eisenhower's proposal, the International Atomic Energy Agency was established in 1957 to "seek to accelerate and enlarge the contribution of atomic energy to peace, health and prosperity throughout the world" and to prevent the misuse of nuclear technology and materials for armaments.

The Baruch Plan, the Atoms for Peace plan and the founding of the IAEA represented three early pillars of an evolving nuclear nonproliferation regime—all attempts to race against the spread of nuclear weapons. The cornerstone of that regime became the Nuclear Non-Proliferation Treaty of 1968 that entered into force in 1970 after some close calls between the superpowers during the 1960s when the Berlin wall crisis of 1961 and the Cuban missile crisis of 1962 brought both countries close to a catastrophic nuclear war. In stepping back from that nuclear abyss, the United States and the Soviet Union realized that the third nuclear race against proliferation merited closer attention.

The NPT remains a centerpiece of that third race, seeking to make nuclear war less likely by preventing the spread of nuclear weapons to other countries. The global "nonproliferation regime," which includes the NPT and other measures, focuses on implementing supply-side "denial strategies" by an array of institutions and policies. Although it clearly has not frozen the membership of the nuclear club, the regime has restrained countries with nuclear ambitions and reinforced an almost universal consensus against the further spread of nuclear weapons.

The NPT represents the most widely adhered-to arms control treaty in history. As of 2006, 188 have signed onto it as parties, including all five permanent members of the UN Security Council (Britain, China, France, Russia and the United States). In signing onto the treaty, these five nuclear weapons states pledged not to help nonnuclear weapons states get the bomb and to facilitate "the fullest possible exchange of equipment, materials and scientific and technological information for the peaceful uses of nuclear energy" (Article IV). Nuclear weapons states also promise to "pursue negotiations in good faith on effective measures relating to cessation of the nuclear arms race at an early date and to nuclear disarmament" (Article VI).

When nonnuclear weapons states become parties to the NPT, they agree not to receive or manufacture nuclear weapons, to accept IAEA "safeguards," a system of accounting

NPT: A Ready Reference
(a summary of major articles)

ARTICLE I Nuclear weapons states pledge not to transfer nuclear explosive devices to any recipient or to assist any nonweapons states to manufacture or otherwise acquire nuclear weapons or other nuclear explosive devices.

ARTICLE II Nonweapons states pledge not to receive nuclear weapons or other nuclear explosive devices or attempt to acquire them.

ARTICLE III Nonweapons states agree to IAEA safeguards—inspection of all nuclear activities and accounting for all nuclear materials.

ARTICLE IV Materials for the production of nuclear energy are excluded from the ban; parties are entitled—and can receive assistance—to use nuclear energy for peaceful purposes.

ARTICLE V The potential benefits of "peaceful nuclear explosions" conducted by weapons states will be made available on a nondiscriminatory basis.

ARTICLE VI The parties to the treaty, particularly

for and monitoring of nuclear materials, and to <u>declare</u> and <u>submit all nuclear materials they own to regular IAEA in-spections</u>. Inspectors verify that nonweapons states have not diverted nuclear materials to military purposes (Article III). The NPT incentive structure lies in the assumption and "nuclear bargain" that nonweapons states will accept access

the nuclear weapons states, pledge to work to-ward "cessation of the nuclear arms race" and universal nuclear disarmament.

ARTICLE VII Regional associations have the right to declare their territories "nuclear-free zones."

ARTICLE VIII Any party may propose an amend-ment to the treaty. When one third of the parties request it, a conference of all parties must be called for the purpose of considering the amend-ment. The treaty will be amended if a majority, including all weapons states party to the treaty (Britain, China, France, Russia and the United States), agree. Treaty-review conferences will be held every five years.

ARTICLE IX A nuclear weapons state is one which has manufactured and exploded a nuclear de-vice prior to January 1, 1967.

ARTICLE X Parties may withdraw from the treaty on three-months notice if they deem their su-preme interests to be jeopardized. A 1995 con-ference determined that the treaty shall con-tinue in force indefinitely.

to civilian nuclear technology in exchange for the verification requirements of IAEA safeguards.

Since 1970, NPT member states have held seven review conferences, one every five years as required by the treaty (Article VIII). At the fifth review conference in 1995, members decided that the NPT shall continue in force indefinitely (Article X).

The seventh review conference held in May 2005, however, ended without a consensus agreement on how to proceed with curbing the spread of nuclear weapons. While three of the previous six review conferences had not reached consensus either, Joseph Cirincione, director for nonproliferation at the Carnegie Endowment for International Peace, testifying to Congress before the last conference, saw this as a failure, "a serious blow to the confidence that all of the other nations have in the nuclear nonproliferation regime." He argued it "will greatly set back our efforts to resolve the crisis of Iran, to resolve the crisis of North Korea, [and] to change the rules of the road on the nuclear fuel cycle."

Congressman Brad Sherman (D-Calif.) noted other sources of friction over U.S. policy at the conference including the Bush Administration's 2002 withdrawal from the 1972 Anti-Ballistic Missile (ABM) Treaty, opposition to ratifying the 1996 Comprehensive Nuclear Test-Ban Treaty (CTBT), adopted by the UN General Assembly, and the development of new nuclear weapons capabilities known as "bunker busters" for potential use against hardened underground terrorist targets or illegal state nuclear activities. In 2000, the Clinton Administration had committed to ratifying the CTBT, preserving the ABM Treaty and 11 other arms control commitments. Jean P. du Preez, director of the nonproliferation program at the Monterey Institute Center for Nonproliferation Studies, said that nonnuclear parties to the NPT remained

unhappy with the lack of U.S. commitment unde
to universal nuclear disarmament.

U.S. Assistant Secretary of State Stephen Rademaker,
head of the arms control bureau, however, argued that NPT
parties needed instead to focus on nonproliferation, and in
particular on Iran and North Korea, countries seeking nuclear weapons, and on greater restrictions and controls over
certain nuclear materials in civilian programs. Linking progress on disarmament to strengthening the NPT's provisions,
Rademaker argued, would weaken nonproliferation efforts
because it would appear to excuse proliferation by blaming
those who lawfully possess nuclear weapons under the NPT.
Moreover, he emphasized that Bush Administration policies,
which include reducing the numbers of nuclear weapons in
the field and the number of warheads, are not drawing the
attention and support they deserve. The United States and
Russia agreed in May 2002 to cut their number of nuclear
warheads by two thirds by 2012, reducing their arsenals to
1,700–2,200 nuclear weapons.

Henry Sokolski, former government official and director
of the Nonproliferation Policy Education Center in Washington, played down the urgency surrounding any NPT consensus document. Ultimately, he argued, success cannot turn
on one statement agreed upon at a four-week conference
in New York City as much as "what we are prepared to do
over the next five years." Among those measures, Sokolski
believes the United States should restrain civilian nuclear
power sales to countries of proliferation concern, citing a deal
by Westinghouse to sell nuclear power plants to China, and
similar discussions with India over reactor sales.

In any case, despite the lack of conference results, the director of the IAEA outlined the challenges facing the NPT,
as well as the third race against proliferation after 9/11. In the

five years since the last review conference, he argued, "The world has changed. Our fears of a deadly nuclear detonation—whatever the cause—have been reawakened. In part, these fears are driven by new realities. The rise in terrorism. The discovery of clandestine nuclear programs. The emergence of a nuclear black market. But these realities have also heightened our awareness of vulnerabilities in the NPT regime....The treaty has served us well for 35 years. But unless we regard it as part of a living, dynamic regime—capable of evolving to match changing realities, it will fade into irrelevance and leave us vulnerable and unprotected."

ElBaradei proposed his seven-step program for keeping the NPT regime alive and well: **(1)** Send a clear-cut message by **recommitting to the original nonproliferation goals.** Have zero tolerance for new states developing nuclear weapons and ensure that all countries have the right to use nuclear technology for peaceful purposes; **(2) Strengthen the IAEA's verification authority** by giving it adequate legal authority, state-of-the-art technology, access to all available information, and sufficient human and financial resources. Beyond verification, the IAEA needs effective export controls, physical protection of nuclear material and mechanisms for dealing with cases of noncompliance; **(3) Establish better control over the nuclear fuel cycle**—both uranium enrichment and plutonium separation—to reduce the chances of proliferation while guaranteeing access to peaceful uses of nuclear technology; **(4) Secure and control nuclear material** by broadening international and regional initiatives and the scope of The International Convention on the Suppression of Acts of Nuclear Terrorism and the Convention on the Physical Protection of Nuclear Material. Moreover, the use of highly enriched uranium in peaceful nuclear applications should be eliminated; **(5) Recommit to nuclear**

Mohamed ElBaradei, director general of the International Atomic Energy Agency, who in a speech on March 25, 2006, reiterated his doubts about Iran's insistence that its atomic plans were purely peaceful. He said that Iran's program "has created a confidence deficit regarding its nature and its direction."

disarmament by holding the nuclear weapons states to their promises and starting disarmament discussions with states not party to the NPT, namely India, Israel and Pakistan; (6) Establish an effective mechanism for dealing with NPT noncompliance through the UN Security Council by taking appropriate measures to deal with noncompliance or withdrawal from the NPT; and (7) Encourage nuclear-weapons-free zones and security assurances in areas such as the Middle East and the Korean peninsula.

In his conclusion, ElBaradei warned about current dangers, and the fourth nuclear race that began after 9/11: "If recent history is any teacher, by 2010, would-be proliferators

Will Terrorists Likely Use a Nuclear Weapon or a Dirty Bomb?

To BUILD A NUCLEAR WEAPON FROM SCRATCH, terrorists would have to overcome enormous technical and logistical obstacles before they could construct then detonate a nuclear bomb on a U.S. city. While terrorists could possibly buy a nuclear weapon, they would still face the challenges of smuggling it into the United States and detonating it. Experts believe a more likely scenario involves terrorist use of a "dirty bomb," also known as a "radiological dispersal device." A dirty bomb is *not* a nuclear

SOURCE: RONALD J. BEE

A Terrorist's Difficult Path to Making and Using a Nuclear Weapon
Objectives, Steps and Challenges

OBJECTIVE # 1
ACQUIRE NUCLEAR WEAPONS FISSILE MATERIAL
Steps: Buy or steal enough highly enriched uranium (HEU) or plutonium from nuclear facilities, storage sites or reactors worldwide (130 research reactors worldwide use HEU).
Challenges: Most nuclear facilities have security measures and low quantities of materials. Thieves have difficulty connecting with customers.
OBJECTIVE # 2
SMUGGLE THE FISSILE MATERIALS TO A SAFE PLACE
Steps: Uranium or plutonium must be removed from facilities, shielded from detection, and transported across borders.
Challenges: Need to hire or bribe numerous people at border crossings, airports and seaports. Lead shielding needed to mask uranium. Plutonium much easier to detect with passive sensors.

weapon. Rather it uses explosives such as dynamite to spread radioactive materials where the bomb detonates. The main harm comes at the point of explosion from the dynamite—nothing compared to the destruction or lethality of a nuclear weapon's blast, heat and radiation. "The good news," according to nuclear terrorist expert Graham Allison, "is that they [dirty bombs] present far less catastrophic threats than true nuclear terrorism. The bad news, however, is that radioactive materials are so widely available in the industrial economies that even a determined effort to deny terrorists access to such material is bound to fail."

OBJECTIVE # 3
BUILD THE NUCLEAR WEAPON
Steps: The most likely method involves building a crude device called a gun-type bomb, using at least 50 kilograms of HEU and conventional explosives.
Challenges: Need expertise in explosives, weapons construction and uranium handling. Need equipment, materials and a facility for assembling the device.

OBJECTIVE # 4
SMUGGLE THE WEAPON INTO THE UNITED STATES
Steps: An oil-tanker hull could protect a nuclear weapon from detection at seaports. Smuggling routes used by drug dealers and illegal immigrant runners could provide a way in.
Challenges: Passive sensors at borders can detect plutonium. A large truck or ship risks inspection.

OBJECTIVE # 5
DETONATE THE NUCLEAR WEAPON
Steps: Conventional explosives can set off a crude device, and a plane can drop a gravity bomb.
Challenges: If bought, sophisticated locking systems require dismantling. If made, terrorists might not risk testing if they only have a small amount of material.

HORIZONTAL NUCLEAR PROLIFERATION AND ROLLBACK

NPT NUCLEAR WEAPONS STATES	DECLARED OR ALLEGED NUCLEAR WEAPONS PROGRAMS	RESTRAINED OR ABANDONED DUE TO MILITARY DEFEAT OR ALLIANCE	NUCLEAR WEAPONS ROLLED BACK DUE TO DIPLOMACY	STATES CAPABLE OF BUT DECIDED NOT TO PURSUE NUCLEAR WEAPONS
Britain China France Russia United States	India Iran Israel North Korea Pakistan	Germany Iraq Japan South Korea Taiwan	Argentina Belarus Brazil Kazakhstan Libya South Africa Ukraine	Australia Canada Egypt Italy Norway Spain Sweden Switzerland

SOURCE: MICHAEL D. YAFFE

will continue to innovate, and sensitive nuclear technology will continue to spread. The arsenals of nuclear weapons states will continue to be modernized. And extremist groups will continue their hunt to acquire and use a nuclear explosive device—or even worse, succeed."

And the Fourth Race—Against Terrorists Acquiring Nuclear Weapons

In October 2003, Italian authorities seized a German ship carrying components for 1,000 high-speed centrifuges (useful for separating U235 from U238) headed to Libya. By December 2003, after the U.S.-led invasion of Iraq, Libyan leader Muammar el-Qaddafi decided to give up his country's nuclear program and cooperate with international inspectors, handing over all of his equipment and a mother lode of information. Documents turned over included centrifuge designs and plans for a nuclear bomb, reportedly wrapped in plastic bags from an Islamabad dry cleaner. The evidence all led to one Dr. A.Q. Khan, the so-called father of Pakistan's nuclear program, who confessed on February 4, 2004, on Pakistani television that he had sold nuclear weapons designs, equipment and materials to Libya, North Korea and Iran. In fact, Khan ran a one-stop shopping "Wal-Mart" of private-sector proliferation with 24-hour technical assistance and even color brochures. He traveled the world for over a decade, visiting countries in Africa, Central Asia and the Middle East.

Khan, now under house arrest in Pakistan, cannot be interrogated by either the United States or the IAEA who would dearly like to know the scope and particulars of all Khan's nuclear yard sales. The United States and the IAEA now suspect that Khan sold North Korea and Iran much of the material they needed to build a bomb, including weapons designs and high speed centrifuges like the ones sold to Libya.

U.S. officials believe private-nuclear-trafficking networks like that run by Khan point to glaring gaps in the NPT regime. Onward proliferation, a new term of proliferation art, refers to proliferators like Khan or other nuclear entrepreneurs sharing or selling their nuclear wares to nuclear aspirants like Libya, North Korea and Iran. Moreover, America's ultimate fearful scenario involves one of Khan's clients, his network, or another network passing along nuclear technology and expertise to terrorist groups. Although the United States does not have specific evidence that links Khan to Al Qaeda, some of Pakistan's military and intelligence units who worked with Khan did sympathize with Osama bin Laden, and reports suggest that Khan had a devout faith that Muslim possession of nuclear weapons would help return Islam to greatness.

Thus far, according to the Nuclear Threat Initiative, the dozens of documented thefts and sales of fissile material to potential terrorists have revealed Russia as a primary source. Russia has large amounts of poorly secured, highly enriched uranium and plutonium that remain a prime target for theft.

September 11 highlighted the dangers that the third nuclear race against proliferation, if not won, could lead to nuclear weapons, materials and know-how falling into the hands of terrorists. In March 2002 testimony before the Senate Armed Services Committee, George Tenet, then director of the Central Intelligence Agency, quoted Al Qaeda leader bin Laden as calling it a "religious duty" for his followers to acquire a nuclear weapon. In 1998 bin Laden issued a statement along these lines in a pamphlet called "The Nuclear Bomb of Islam" and also threatened that "America will see its own Hiroshima." Documents found in Al Qaeda caves during the post-9/11 war in Afghanistan also suggested its direct interest in nuclear devices for eventual use against the United States.

2

The Axis of Upheaval:
Iraq, Iran and North Korea

IN HIS 2002 STATE OF THE UNION ADDRESS, the first after 9/11, President Bush called Iraq, Iran and North Korea the "axis of evil," accusing these states of seeking nuclear weapons, whose sale or transfer to terrorists would directly threaten the United States. In so doing, the President proclaimed a major focus—if not the major focus—of his Administration was to protect the United States from terrorists, and by extension, those states that harbor them or could supply them with WMD. "We'll be deliberate, yet time is not on our side," the President said. "I will not wait on events, while dangers gather. I will not stand by, as peril draws closer and closer."

This first meant invading Afghanistan (Operation Enduring Freedom) to root out the Al Qaeda network and topple the Taliban regime that had sponsored Al Qaeda and its training camps within its borders. It also signaled a proactive global war on terrorism abroad and the establishment of the Department of Homeland Security (DHS) at home. Virtually no one, including the UN, argued against attacking those responsible for 9/11 in Afghanistan as a matter of self-defense and as a response sanctioned by international law. The North Atlantic Treaty Organization (NATO), for the first time in its history, unanimously invoked Article V of its charter to come to the aid of an alliance member, the United States.

The debate began and remains around the notion that the United States and its allies, when necessary, could or should attack countries like Iraq, Iran and North Korea before they attack us or help a terrorist attack us. On June 1, 2002, the President clarified his views on the need for preemption to protect U.S. national interests in a post-9/11 threat environment. At West Point's graduation exercises, he argued that "for much of the last century, America's defense relied on the cold-war doctrines of deterrence and containment.... But new threats also require new thinking. Deterrence— the promise of massive retaliation against nations—means nothing against shadowy terrorist networks with no nation or citizens to defend. Containment is not possible when unbalanced dictators with WMD can deliver those weapons on missiles or secretly provide them to terrorist allies....We must take the battle to the enemy, disrupt his plans, and confront the worst threats before they emerge." President Bush then asserted to the cadets, "Our security will require all Americans to be forward-looking and resolute, to be ready for preemptive action when necessary to defend our liberty and to defend our lives."

Three Strikes and You're Out

After 9/11, the Bush Administration clearly thought that preemptive action fitted the bill for Iraq. Yet the idea let alone action of "preemptive nonproliferation" by military attack did not start with the current Bush Administration. Three important sequential military operations played a role in preempting Saddam's nuclear ambitions directly or indirectly, over three decades, by design or by accident: Operation Babylon (Israel's 1981 unilateral action, by design); Operation Desert Storm (U.S.-led UN coalition in 1991, by accident); and Operation Iraqi Freedom (U.S.-led "coalition of the willing," in 2003, by design). The Iran-Iraq war (1980–88) also saw intermittent Iranian air attacks against Iraqi nuclear facilities. The 1981 Israeli attack and the Iranian raids drove Saddam's WMD programs underground and out of the UN's eye until Operation Desert Storm in 1991, conducted ostensibly to drive Saddam out of Kuwait. Quite by chance, allied troops found secret and illegal WMD programs in Iraq along the way, and over the next 10 years, through the UN, disarming those programs started. After 9/11, another decade later, under the George W. Bush Administration, Iraq became another battle in the global war on terrorism, whose major rationale centered on Iraq continuing its secret WMD programs in defiance of 17 UN Security Council resolutions. While this third and final operation found no WMD, it did oust Saddam Hussein from power, thus ending any residual ambitions or plans he might have had for acquiring them, let alone sharing them with terrorists.

Operation Babylon

On Sunday June 7, 1981, eight Israeli F-16 Falcon aircraft escorted by six F-15s took off from their Sinai Peninsula base laden with MK-84 gravity bombs for a secret more than 600-mile-long operation to destroy the Osirak nuclear reactor at Tuwaitha, 12 miles outside Baghdad. In the 1970s, France had agreed with Saddam Hussein to build an Osiris nuclear "research" reactor, a huge aluminum-domed, top-of-the-line reactor named for the Egyptian god of the underworld. France also supplied Iraq with 12.5 kilograms of highly enriched weapons-grade uranium 235. By mid-summer of 1981, Saddam Hussein's heavily defended nuclear facility would go online and start producing weapons-grade plutonium that could furnish Iraq with enough fissile material for two or three Hiroshima-size bombs a year. Israel knew it would become one of Saddam's nuclear targets; Iraq had pledged to destroy the Jewish state.

Operation Babylon, code-named for the biblical name of Iraq and planned as a "black operation" for over two years, successfully destroyed the Osirak reactor on June 7, 1981. All pilots returned safely, having flown undetected over Jordanian, Saudi and Iraqi territory. Iraq, at war with Iran at the time, could not easily strike back at Israel. While Israel took plenty of international criticism and condemnation for the destruction of Osirak, the raid did set back Iraq's nuclear program by several years. The raid did not, however, destroy the scientific expertise. Saddam Hussein had learned not to put all of his nuclear activities in one centerpiece facility, or in plain view. The Israeli attack only made him more determined to get the bomb. Dr. Khidhir Hamza, a former Iraqi nuclear scientist, said, after the raid on Osirak, "We went from 500 people to 7,000, in a timeframe of five years. All done in secret." So Saddam nodded once again to Osiris, and began secretly building a vast underground nuclear weapons program only discovered and destroyed 10 years later, this time largely by accident.

Operation Desert Storm

On August 2, 1990, Iraq invaded neighboring Kuwait and overthrew the government of the late Sheikh Jaber al-Sabah. Iraq annexed Kuwait as its "19th province," claiming it rightfully belonged to Iraq, as proven by the original borders of the Ottoman Empire. The British, Iraqis claimed, unfairly drew the Iraq-Kuwait border in 1922 so as to deny Iraq access to the Persian Gulf. Moreover, Kuwait had stolen oil from Iraq's Rumailia oil field, overproduced oil in violation of the Organization of the Petroleum Exporting Countries quotas and lowered the price of oil, thus "destroying Iraq's economy." Four days later, in response to the invasion, the UN Security Council enacted mandatory trade and financial sanctions against Iraq, thus shutting down 98 percent of Iraq's oil exports and 95 percent of its imports. Shortly after invading Kuwait, Iraqi forces made several raids into Saudi Arabia. Days later, then Secretary of Defense Richard Cheney showed Saudi King Fahd U.S. satellite photos of 250,000 Iraqi troops and ground-to-ground missiles allegedly assembling on his border. Saudi King Fahd asked the United States to deploy troops to Saudi Arabia to deter an Iraqi invasion.

The same day, President George H. W. Bush (1989–93) defined U.S. policy objectives: secure unconditional withdrawal of all Iraqi forces from Kuwait; restore Kuwait's legitimate government; maintain the security and stability of the

Persian Gulf region; and protect U.S. citizens. On November 29, the UN Security Council authorized force if Iraq did not withdraw from Kuwait by January 15, 1991. Iraq refused to comply and on January 16, 1991, Operation Desert Storm began with an extensive air war. The air war, quite by accident, started unveiling Saddam's secret nuclear programs.

As the air war's dust settled, bombing assessment photos began revealing puzzling data that later made it clear secret nuclear weapons laboratories had been hit. A lucky F-117 pilot, running low on fuel, dropped his last bomb on a target that his map called a Tuwaitha administration building that actually destroyed a secret laboratory crucial to recasting uranium fuel into a nuclear explosive. Stealth bombers, in their last sortie of the war, hit Saddam's Al Atheer weapons-design center, listed as an unfinished factory that the analysts could not quite decipher, put on the target list because it lay close to the Iraqi army's high-explosive testing centers at Al Qa Qaa and Al Hatteen. An F-14 Tomcat used a ground-buster bomb to attack the Tarmiya complex just north of Baghdad, designated a Grade B target that analysts presumed was a munitions factory. The bomb peeled back the roof of the factory like the lid of a sardine can and exposed something altogether fishy that looked like rows of giant frisbees. For weeks analysts scratched their heads over the aerial photographs. Finally, a retired U.S. nuclear physicist, John Gogain, gave them the answer after glimpsing at them. "My God, that's Oak Ridge, Tennessee, where I worked all my life." When told these pictures came from Iraq, he explained that the frisbees actually represented vast calutron magnets used to separate out weapons-grade uranium.

On February 23, the ground war began with U.S. Marines, U.S. Army and UN coalition forces. Four days later, Kuwait was liberated. On March 3, 2001, the leaders of

Feb. 7, 1992: A USAF A-10A Thunderbolt II aircraft flies over a target area during Operation Desert Storm. The plane was designed especially for close air support of ground forces.

Iraq formally accepted the cease-fire terms offered to them.

Later revelations made by Lt. Gen. Hussein Kamel, former Iraqi minister of industry and military industrialization, after his defection to Jordan on August 8, 1995, informed the IAEA that Saddam had ordered a crash nuclear program following the invasion of Kuwait in 1990. The program sought the accelerated design and construction of an implosion-type nuclear weapon, the building of a test site in Kuwait, and development of a delivery vehicle—with a deadline of April 1991. Operation Desert Storm, the second strike against Saddam's WMD programs, fortunately happened when it did.

Instead of a nuclear weapon, Iraq received UN Security Council Resolution 687 in April 1991, following its defeat in Operation Desert Storm, which further curtailed its nuclear aspirations and started the dismantling of its WMD programs. The combination of military operations and the subsequent inspection and dismantling efforts of the IAEA, assisted by the UN Special Commission (UNSCOM), rid Iraq of weapons-capable fissile material and nuclear weapons production facilities. Nevertheless, Saddam insisted on preserving many of his WMD-related capabilities, despite UN resolutions, and actively hindered the UN inspection process throughout the 1990s. That obstinacy and the resulting UN economic sanctions cost Iraq an estimated $140 billion in oil revenues—a very high price tag for keeping the vestiges of Iraq's weapons infrastructure intact.

By the fall of 1998, Saddam had grown more defiant and would only allow inspectors access to suspect facilities if the UN ended economic sanctions. By December 15, Richard Butler, the UNSCOM chief, reported that "Iraq's conduct ensured that no progress was able to be made in the fields of disarmament." This led to the withdrawal of all UN inspectors the next day, followed by a joint U.S.-British military action, Operation Desert Fox, the next evening. Saddam still refused to allow UN inspectors back in. UN Security Council Resolution 1284, adopted in December 1999, established a follow-on inspection regime under the UN Monitoring, Verification and Inspection Commission (UNMOVIC), to continue UNSCOM's work. Saddam continued to play "hide and seek" with UNMOVIC, which stopped its operations just prior to Operation Desert Storm in March 2003.

Operation Iraqi Freedom

According to Bob Woodward's book, *Plan of Attack* (Simon & Schuster, 2004), in the immediate aftermath of 9/11, with dust and smoke still filling the operations center of the Pen-

June 9, 2003: A Bradley Fighting Vehicle passes a UN inspector from the International Atomic Energy Agency as he tries to assess Iraq's nuclear facility in Tuwaitha, 31 miles east of Baghdad, which was looted during the U.S.-led invasion.

AP/WIDE WORLD PHOTOS

tagon, Secretary of Defense Rumsfeld raised with his staff the possibility of going after Iraq as a response to the terrorist attacks. On September 16 at Camp David, four of the President's top advisers, with Rumsfeld abstaining, voted against hitting Iraq first. Afghanistan, as the known safe harbor for Al Qaeda, made more sense. Iraq, however, remained on the table. President Bush told Dr. Rice, then his national security adviser, "We won't do Iraq now. We're putting Iraq off. But eventually we'll have to return to that question."

By September 2002, the White House clearly had returned to it, setting its preemptive sights on Iraq when it unveiled the National Security Strategy (NSS) of the United States. Building upon the June 2002 West Point "preemption" speech, the strategy states, "At the time of the Gulf War [1991], we acquired irrefutable proof that Iraq's designs were not limited to the chemical weapons it had used against Iran and its own people, but also extended to the acquisition of nuclear weapons and biological agents."

Containing terrorism meant moving beyond conventional deterrence. After the first phase in Afghanistan, the second phase involved confronting the WMD activities of the axis of evil, with the first stop in Iraq. All of America's traditional allies agreed with phase one; most in fact had citizens that died on 9/11. Not all agreed with phase two, which required acting before an actual terrorist attack occurred. On January 28, 2003, in the State of the Union address, President Bush stated, "If Saddam Hussein does not fully disarm, for the safety of our people and for the peace of the world, we will lead a coalition to disarm him."

On February 5, 2003, Secretary of State Colin Powell presented evidence to the UN Security Council that Iraq had concealed WMD in defiance of 12 years of UN sanctions and 17 UN Security Council resolutions. Not all agreed. A row emerged publicly over removing Saddam by force. The United States and Britain said yes. France, Germany, Belgium and Russia said no, pushing instead for more time for IAEA inspectors to verify earlier Iraqi WMD declarations made to the UN. For President Bush, however, unverified Iraqi declarations rang hollow in the shadow of 9/11, while "regime change" resonated well with his proactive approach to thwarting terrorism. Under Article 51 of the UN Charter, states can act in self-defense if an armed attack occurs. Moreover, the United States had already interpreted 17 UN

Security Council resolutions as authorizing the use of force.

The debate ended on March 19, 2003, when the United States, with a "coalition of the willing," launched Operation Iraqi Freedom. Worries about WMD, including nuclear weapons, had pushed the United States into action. Major military actions in Iraq ended within a month and a half, and over 130,000 American and coalition troops now stand guard over that country as it reorganizes its daily life and government. With Saddam now in custody and awaiting trial, attacks from regime remnants and sympathizers occur often against coalition troops, against Iraqis working with them, and against innocent Iraqis.

After three years of coalition presence in Iraq, the United States still has not found any significant quantities of WMD. David Kay, the former top U.S. weapons inspector for Unscom, first led the Iraqi Survey Group (ISG), created by the CIA in May 2003, to look for Iraqi WMD. While some 1,400 inspectors searched high and low for WMD, and did find evidence of "WMD program-related activities," Kay stepped down before the investigation finished, concluding in his parting Senate testimony on January 28, 2004, that "we were almost all wrong," blaming the Iraq WMD assumptions on bad international intelligence.

For opponents of Operation Iraqi Freedom, and even some supporters like Senator John McCain (R-Ariz.), this issue raised questions about whether the President somehow misled the American people and the U.S. Congress into supporting the war. Given the Administration's claims, many Americans thought the U.S. government should have known the location of at least some Iraqi WMD. The President, however, remained resolute in supporting the invasion, saying that "Saddam Hussein's regime is a grave and gathering danger" to America and the world. That may have been true, but it was not because of his current WMD programs in Iraq.

Kay stated that "to date we have not uncovered evidence that Iraq undertook significant post-1998 steps to actually build nuclear weapons or produce fissile material." He had "no doubt" that Iraq had less ability to produce fissile material than it had in 1991. Saddam's program "had been seriously degraded. The activities of the inspectors in the early 1990s did a tremendous amount." Charles A. Duelfer, Kay's replacement, finished the CIA investigation and his conclusions did not differ from Kay's, as well as those of Hans Blix, former head of the UN's UNMOVIC that conducted international inspections for WMD in Iraq from 2000 until March 2003. Blix said in 2003 he believed Iraq had destroyed most of its WMD years before but kept up the appearance that it had them to deter any military attack. Blix wrote a book in 2004 called *Disarming Iraq* (Pantheon) that describes his experience at UNMOVIC. When he gave a keynote address at the 2004 annual Carnegie Endowment for International Peace nonproliferation conference in Washington, Blix opened his remarks with the wry hint of a smile, saying "I am glad to note that my book *Disarming Iraq* still remains on the nonfiction list."

Anthony H. Cordesman, security analyst at the Washington-based Center for Strategic and International Studies sees it this way: "The Bush Administration overplayed the WMD card but if the UN had lifted economic sanctions, Saddam would have gladly picked up the pieces of his programs and tried again." In a post-9/11 world, Saddam Hussein created a "WMD ambiguity" that ultimately cost him his regime.

Iran: Squeeze Play

On Inauguration Day, January 20, 2005, Vice President Cheney told a radio talk show host that "Iran is right at the

Satellite image of the Natanz nuclear facility in Iran,
the existence of which was revealed by Iranian dissidents in August
2002. UN inspectors have found traces of highly enriched,
weapons-grade uranium at this site.

top of the list" for the Bush Administration. He harked back
to the 1981 Israeli Osirak raid against Iraq, saying "the Israelis might well decide to act first, and let the rest of the world
worry about cleaning up the diplomatic mess afterward." The

Aug. 16, 2005: One of hundreds of Iranian students rallying in support of Iran's nuclear program outside the gates of the Isfahan uranium conversion plant, just south of Tehran.

nuclear energy
is our
obvious right

Vice President, when secretary of defense during the U.S. strike on Iraq in 1991, reportedly gave a photograph of the Osirak reactor to the Israeli general who had commanded the Israeli air force during that raid with a note that said "With thanks and appreciation for the outstanding job he did on the Iraqi nuclear program in 1981, which made our job much easier in Desert Storm." In any case, now that the third strike against Iraq has deposed Saddam Hussein, clearly Iran lays squarely on President Bush's nuclear nonproliferation agenda.

The Bush Administration remains keen on convincing

Iran to end its extensive nuclear activities for many reasons. For starters, Iran possesses huge reserves of oil. Why should it develop nuclear energy sources? Second, Iran shares an 800-mile border with Iraq, where 130,000 U.S. troops now help one of Iran's biggest enemies it fought from 1980 to 1988 become a self-governing state and a beacon for political reforms in the region. The United States and the fledgling Iraqi government do not want Iran meddling in Iraqi internal affairs or Iran's radical mullahs, emboldened by a nuclear capability, creating more targets. Third, Iran also shares a border with Afghanistan, yet another nation where U.S. troops have a considerable presence, there are radical Islamist troubles and a fledgling democracy struggles to survive. Fourth, many experts believe that one of the biggest challenges the U.S.-backed Roadmap for Peace in the Middle East faces are spoilers like Hezbollah, a radical Muslim group in Lebanon, that Iran and Syria have reportedly supported with weapons, money and ideology to fight and conduct terrorist attacks against Israel. Will an emboldened nuclear Iran cause more or less trouble for Israel? And last but not least, a nuclear Iran might wish to share its secrets, materials or weaponry with like-minded terrorists—a doomsday scenario the United States wants to thwart.

Iran, however, also learned from the Osirak 1981 raid and dispersed its nuclear assets and activities across the country and in some underground, unknown locations. This in itself complicates any consideration of a quick-fix Osirak-type military attack. Does the United States really want to wage another war, replace another regime, and occupy another country where it would remain very unwelcome, a country with over 70 million proud inhabitants who would likely resist? Would Iran defend itself with its conventional military forces or widen the conflict by attacking Iraq or perhaps shutting down the Strait of Hormuz—a key shipping choke point for Persian Gulf oil?

The Iranian nuclear weapons program began in earnest in 1974 when Shah Mohammad Reza Pahlavi concluded that having a nuclear capability would ensure his ability to dictate his nation's future. Under an agreement made by President Richard M. Nixon with the shah in May 1972, the United States agreed to sell Iran any conventional weapon, short of nuclear arms. The Islamic Revolution of 1979 ended the shah's nuclear ambitions for Iran, and the Iran-Iraq war that began in 1980 did not make a nuclear weapons program cost-effective or politically feasible, at least until 1984. Iraqi air raids in 1987 and 1988 halted the program again by damaging Iranian reactor sites at Bushehr I and II.

Over the next 15 years, Iran secretly sought to build its nuclear capabilities. Gary Sick, executive director of the Gulf/2000 Project at Columbia University, has written, "The pattern of known Iranian nuclear purchases, the stealth it displayed in pursuing some of its contacts, the weapons-related nature of some of its attempted purchases, and the absence of any compelling rationale for an immensely expensive nuclear power program in a country with abundant conventional energy resources, all suggest the international community is right to be suspicious of Iran's intentions."

By the fall of 2003, with Saddam Hussein's regime gone, and North Korea already in six-party talks, Iran became the next nuclear villain on the "axis of evil" target list. The IAEA, prompted by the United States, demanded Iran clarify its nuclear intentions, stop its nuclear activities, and suspend all efforts to make nuclear weapons. Iran faced possible international sanctions and U.S. military action if it did not comply by October 31. On October 21, Iran met with the foreign ministers of France, Germany and Britain and agreed with

IRANium

the IAEA's demands. Since that time, France, Germany and Britain have conducted EU-3 negotiations with Iran. These talks employ a "carrot and stick" approach, offering political and economic incentives in exchange for the freezing of nuclear activities and ultimately their cessation. While the United States has been supporting the talks with Iran, those talks have required the U.S. threat of force as "the stick behind the carrot." Although France, Germany and Britain can provide Iran the tactical benefits, the strategic benefits must come from a U.S. security guarantee because Iran, with American forces on two of its borders, sees Washington as its greatest security threat.

The United States isn't likely to ever give that guarantee unless Iran gives up its nuclear activities, can verify their end with international inspections, and stops its support for terrorist groups like Hezbollah in Lebanon, and Hamas and Islamic Jihad in the Palestinian territories. Iran has opposed the Middle East peace process since its inception in 1991 and has financially supported and trained terrorist groups as "spoilers" of that process.

Patrick Clawson, deputy director for research of the Washington Institute for Near East Policy, calls Iran "the poster

"HEY, WE'RE ONLY SELLING NUCLEAR FUEL TO IRAN... WE DON'T TELL THEM HOW TO USE IT."

child for the nexus of terrorism and WMD." He argues that Iran, once it had acquired nuclear weapons, would become tempted to share them with terrorists. "After all, mass casualty terrorism done by proxies has worked well for Iran to date. Iranian assistance to the terrorists who blew up the U.S. and French barracks in Beirut in 1983 was a grand strategic success, forcing the United States, and for a while France, out of Lebanon while not bringing any retaliation down on Iran. Similarly, the 1996 bombing of the Khobar Towers barracks in Saudi Arabia caused the Saudis to make a strategic reconciliation, and, once again, Iran faced no retaliation."

Shahram Chubin, director of research at the Geneva Center for Security Studies, and Robert S. Litwak, director of international studies at the Woodrow Wilson International Center for Scholars, have cautioned that "Iran presents conditions that warrant a different policy from those applied to the other two members of the 'axis of evil.'" The authors noted public opinion polls indicating 70 percent of Iranians seek normalization of relations with the United States and engagement with the global community. They believe that "Iran's dynamic domestic politics present an avenue for influencing the country's decisionmaking about its nuclear program."

In February 2003, the IAEA director, ElBaradei, went to Iran with inspectors and discovered that Iran's ruling hardliners did not apparently share that sentiment. They had introduced uranium hexafluoride into gas centrifuges, a clear violation of the NPT. By June 2003, ElBaradei reported to the IAEA that "Iran has failed to meet its obligations under its Safeguards Agreement with respect to the reporting of nuclear material." The IAEA found two different types of highly enriched uranium undeclared by Iran, another clear violation of the NPT. In fact, by November 2003, the IAEA had learned and publicly stated that Iran had systematically lied to it for 18 years about its secret nuclear activities. The report listed nine separate counts of Iran's failure to comply with the NPT. Yet another member of the axis of evil had used the veil of the NPT to feign nonproliferation while covering its nuclear aspirations, or worse, use the NPT as a way to gain the technology and materials it needed to develop a nuclear weapons capability.

By mid-2005, the EU-3 negotiations with Iran had produced precious little, and Tehran was still insisting it would never give up its right to manufacture nuclear fuel. In June 2005 Iran had admitted to yet another set of plutonium experiments it had never reported to the IAEA.

In July 2005, as reported by *The New York Times*, senior U.S. intelligence officials went to Vienna, Austria, to present the IAEA with what it considered clear evidence from a stolen laptop computer that Iran had plans for building a nuclear weapon. The laptop contained over a thousand pages of Iranian computer simulations and accounts of experiments that signaled a determination to build a nuclear warhead, "including a telltale sphere of detonators to trigger an atomic explosion." While the evidence did not prove that Iran has a nuclear weapon, the documents presented strong proof that Tehran seeks to build a compact warhead for its Shahab missile, with a range that could reach Israel and other countries in the Middle East.

On January 12, 2006, the Europeans called off their talks with Tehran, saying Iran should be referred to the UN Security Council. Iran had removed IAEA monitored seals on nuclear facilities involved in the enrichment of uranium, prompting German Foreign Minister Frank-Walter Steinmeier to announce in Berlin, "Our talks with Iran have reached a dead end." On February 4, 2006, the IAEA did just that, with a 27–3 vote that included a united front of France, Germany, Britain, the United States, Russia and China.

Diplomacy still has a chance to work, but past experience with Tehran and the present intransigence of Iran's president may dash those hopes. Russian President Putin has asked that Tehran accept Moscow's offer to move Iran's uranium enrichment program to Russia—a step supported by the United States and its allies. If diplomacy fails, the international UN squeeze play includes a range of options, from economic sanctions to military action. Debates over sanctions will reoccur—whether to use "smart sanctions" aimed at the Iranian leadership and not the people of Iran, whether to embargo Iranian oil exports which could have the effect of expediting Iran's quest for a bomb rather than thwart it, and whether surgical military strikes can achieve what diplomacy cannot. It may mean picking the best of bad strategic options.

Henry A. Kissinger, former secretary of state, has written, "It is possible—even likely—that Iran views its negotiations with the European countries as a way to gain time, perhaps through the second Bush Administration. Iran may well maneuver for a position from which there is only a short final step to a nuclear weapons program, in the meantime encouraging as many incentives of long-term usefulness to the Iranian economy and nuclear program as it can induce the Western negotiators to offer." Kissinger concluded that a nonproliferation policy must "achieve clarity" on a number of issues, or "failure will usher in a new set of nuclear perils dwarfing those which we have just surmounted." He believes it is necessary to first clarify the urgency of timing, tactics and the ultimate purpose of negotiations: "How much time is available before Iran has a nuclear weapons capability, and what strategy can best stop an Iranian nuclear weapons program? How do we prevent the diplomatic process from turning into a means to legitimize proliferation rather than avert it?"

Barring regime change from within, one that assumes a more democratic Iran won't want nuclear weapons, how can Iran be encouraged not to go nuclear?

A Libyan Model for Denuclearization?

Clearly the Bush Administration would prefer an outcome in Iran, and for that matter, North Korea, that looks like what occurred in Libya. In March 2003, during Operation Iraqi Freedom, Libya made quiet overtures to Britain and the United States about coming clean on all its WMD programs. Libya's leader, Colonel Muammar el-Qaddafi, clearly feared his country would soon become one of the next states in the Bush Administration crosshairs for "regime change" due to illicit WMD activities. Moreover, Libya's aging and eccentric leader apparently also worried about the economic legacy he would leave for future Libyan generations if he could sell little oil—let alone tap new deposits or make repairs to oil rigs—due to international sanctions and trade restrictions placed on his country. As a result of Libya's and Iran's role in and support for international terrorism, President Bill Clinton (1993–2001), in 1996, had signed the Iran and Libya Sanctions Act (ILSA) that imposed sanctions on foreign investment in Iran and Libya's energy sectors. President George W. Bush renewed ILSA for another five years on August 3, 2001.

According to Paula A. DeSutter, U.S. Assistant Secretary for Verification and Compliance, in testimony on February 26, 2004, before the Senate Foreign Relations Committee, the United States and Britain "worked together very closely" in secret talks with Libya starting in March 2003, and Libya

Libya's leader, Colonel Muammar el-Qaddafi, stands in front of a statue of a hand catching a U.S. warplane near his home in Tripoli in 2001. By December 2003 Qaddafi had agreed to abandon Libya's clandestine nuclear weapons program in exchange for pledges from Washington and London to lift sanctions. The revelations provided by the Libyans gave Washington the ammunition to force Pakistan's president to put the Khan nuclear network out of business.

began spilling information about its nuclear as well as chemical weapons and ballistic missile programs. In October 2003, the U.S., British, German and Italian governments worked together to intercept a shipment of centrifuge components bound for Libya, secretly bought from the Pakistani nuclear-black-market network of A. Q. Khan. Libya blew the whistle on this network, and in so doing provided a treasure trove of intelligence information on nuclear trafficking.

71

On December 19, 2003, the White House released a fact sheet that announced that Libya, as a direct result of talks with Britain and the United States, had pledged, along with provisions concerning chemical weapons and ballistic missiles, to eliminate all elements of its nuclear weapons programs; declare all nuclear activities to the IAEA; accept international inspections to ensure Libya's complete adherence to the NPT, and allow immediate inspector visits and monitoring to verify all of these actions. The statement went on to declare, "Libya's announcement today is a product of the President's strategy which gives regimes a choice. They can choose to pursue WMD at great peril, cost and international isolation. Or they can choose to renounce these weapons, take steps to rejoin the international community, and have our help in creating a better future for their citizens.... Leaders who abandon the pursuit of chemical, biological and nuclear weapons—and the means to deliver them—will find an open path to better relations with the United States and other free nations."

DeSutter said that Libya had already shown to U.S. and British experts "the substances, equipment and programs," including centrifuges for uranium enrichment, detailed nuclear weapons designs, nuclear weapons components, missiles and nuclear materials. It had also relinquished five SCUD-C guidance sets that indicated extensive assistance from North Korea on missile development, as well as enriched uranium that was traced to Pakistan. All told, Libya loaded some 55,000 pounds of sensitive nuclear items, centrifuge equipment and other materials onto a large U.S. cargo aircraft in Tripoli that flew safely to Tennessee, with another 500 metric tons of cargo piled onto a ship that sailed to North Carolina. All the Libyan nuclear contraband eventually arrived safely at the Department of Energy's Oak Ridge National Laboratory (ORNL) in Tennessee, one of the original nuclear weapons laboratories built for the U.S. Manhattan Project. On March 15, 2004, then Secretary of Energy Spencer Abraham proudly displayed the evidence to journalists.

In her testimony, DeSutter emphasized, "this is one of those rare times that a state has volunteered to rid itself of its WMD programs—and it is a first for a state sponsor of terror to do so without regime change." In closing, she emphasized, "We only hope that states with even more advanced nuclear weapons programs like Iran and North Korea will learn from Libya's example and agree to rejoin the community of civilized nations and give up these terrible weapons."

Thus far, however, both Iran and North Korea have apparently learned the exact opposite—that to protect their repressive regimes, they must deter attack by building nuclear weapons as soon as possible via technology legally acquired by way of the NPT and illegally via black market networks,

Nuclear weapons still found on the menu of the hungry population of North Korea

PEP//CARTOONISTS & WRITERS SYNDICATE/cartoonweb.com

73

buy time and concessions through multilateral negotiations that also help their technicians achieve a weapons capacity, and ignore their NPT obligations that require abandoning those very capacities. Both countries may have learned that they can get more political and economic "carrots" if they first develop their own nuclear "stick," a stick that they perceive may act as a force equalizer against superior American conventional forces.

North Korea: Déjà Vu?

North Korea had already learned in the 1990s that its Communist regime could get away with violating its NPT obligations with impunity. From 1992 to 1994, in what Clinton government officials have called "the most serious nuclear crisis the world had experienced since the superpower confrontation over Soviet missiles in Cuba some three decades earlier," the United States and North Korea almost went to war.

Pyongyang had signed the NPT in 1985, but did not permit IAEA inspections until 1992. When inspectors arrived, they found discrepancies in North Korea's initial declaration of nuclear material—North Korea had produced more plutonium than it had acknowledged. The DPRK then prevented IAEA inspectors from conducting crucial tests needed to verify that no nuclear materials had been diverted from seven declared nuclear sites. In February 1993, the North Koreans denied inspectors access to two undeclared sites suspected of storing nuclear waste products. On March 12, claiming that the IAEA demands violated its national sovereignty, North Korea declared its intention to withdraw from the NPT (a three-month process). On April 1, 1993, the IAEA Board of Governors declared North Korea in noncompliance with the NPT. In May, the UN Security Council passed a resolution

North Korea's spent nuclear fuel rods kept in a cooling pond at Yongbyon. On February 10, 2005, the DPRK announced publicly for the first time that it had nuclear weapons—which it needs as protection against an increasingly hostile United States.

urging North Korea to revoke its withdrawal from the NPT and allow inspections. North Korea refused.

By June 1993, the first round of talks between North Korean and U.S. representatives began in New York City. The United States, according to U.S. negotiators present, hoped to talk down North Korea from its defiant nuclear posture as the "least worst alternative" among choices that included military action, containment through isolation, or forcing North Korea's collapse. When the talks stalled in the spring of 1994, the United States looked seriously at war plans for an air strike against North Korean nuclear facilities, while also seeking sanctions against North Korea from the UN Security Council. North Korean rhetoric intensified, warning that sanctions would amount to an act of war. In discussions with South Koreans, one North Korean diplomat threatened to turn their capital city, Seoul, into a "sea of flames."

Unlike the two desert wars fought in Iraq, a second Korean war would begin just 30 miles from the seat of government and economic center of a key American ally. Two thirds of North Korea's army of over one million soldiers stay deployed within 100 miles of Seoul, and 10 million South Koreans live within artillery range of the North. Some 29,500 American troops remain deployed in South Korea. Any "surgical strike" could prove very costly if it provoked general armed conflict—by some estimates one million casualties could occur in South Korea alone. And those figures pale if the North Koreans have and decide to use nuclear weapons. U.S. negotiators believed, "if war came, it would be another Korean War, not another Gulf war."

Former Secretary of Defense William Perry (1994–97) later concluded that North Korea saw how the American military devastated Iraq twice on the battlefield and in no way can fathom protecting its regime against America without nuclear weapons. "The North Korean military understands quite clearly that they cannot compete with the U.S. military," Perry argues. "Therefore, they argue that they need nuclear weapons as an offset to our preponderant conventional military capability."

In its negotiations, the Clinton Administration used "carrots and sticks," betting that the North Koreans might trade away their bombs—or at least their capacity to build them—in exchange for diplomatic recognition and economic assistance. Some critics, however, argued that these incentives probably meant little to the leaders of an isolated country who remain aloof from world opinion. By continuing to negotiate, they said, the United States risked elevating the value of the North Korean nuclear card. Kim Il Sung, the dictator who had ruled North Korea since 1948, surely sought to test a theory that says nothing makes Washington take you seriously faster than a pile of plutonium.

The first North Korean nuclear crisis peaked from April to June 1994 when the DPRK unloaded 8,000 fuel rods full of plutonium from its five-megawat nuclear reactor in Yongbyong without IAEA supervision. Secretary Perry believed that the fuel from this reactor contained enough plutonium to build four or five nuclear weapons. By mid-June, the United States pressed for sanctions at the UN, deployed more American military forces to the Korean peninsula and reportedly provided 48 Patriot missiles to South Korea to protect against possible North Korean missile attacks.

As tensions mounted, former President Jimmy Carter (1977–81) made a "private visit" (June 15–18), funded by American foundations, to North Korea to seek ways to reopen negotiations with Kim Il Sung. Carter correctly feared war was imminent, and from the North Korean capital, after six hours of discussions, announced on CNN that Pyongyang would allow inspectors back in and stop the plutonium processing. The plot thickened when Kim Il Sung died on July 8, 1994, and his son Kim Jong Il succeeded his father. Talks between the United States and North Korea resumed in August 1994. On October 21, President Clinton approved an accord called the Agreed Framework, whereby North Korea would receive $4 billion in energy aid over the next 10 years in exchange for a commitment to freeze and eventually dismantle its nuclear weapons programs under IAEA supervision. A consortium of nations led by South Korea and Japan would build two light-water nuclear reactors designed to make the conversion of nuclear waste into nuclear weapons more difficult. The consortium agreed to supply fuel oil shipments to North Korea while the reactors got built. The North Koreans had to allow full and continuous inspections of their nuclear sites, suspend construction of two new nuclear reactors, dismantle some of their key nuclear plants, and ship all but 8,000 of their spent nuclear fuel rods out of the country.

The Agreed Framework, along with President Carter's impromptu diplomacy, in the short-term prevented a possible catastrophic war. It also slowed North Korea's production of plutonium while providing some confidence in the broader nonproliferation regime at a critical time when the NPT had come up for indefinite renewal in 1995. But for the long-term, the Agreed Framework clearly did not end North Korea's nuclear ambitions—ambitions that gained new importance when the theory of catastrophic terrorism became a reality after 9/11.

Since October 2002, North Korea has admitted to a new secret uranium enrichment plant, expelled IAEA inspectors again from its Yongbyon plutonium-producing reactor and declared its withdrawal from the NPT again. On February 10, 2005, it declared that it had built nuclear weapons, and in April 2005 it announced once more its withdrawal of the 8,000 fuel rods from the Yongbyon reactor, this time "to increase its nuclear deterrent." North Korea claims that its nuclear weapons programs amount to a defensive response to a hostile Bush Administration that has called it bad names—a member of the axis of evil, an outpost of tyranny—and ridiculed its Supreme Leader, calling Kim Jong Il a "pigmy who starves his own people." North Korea's nuclear weapons program, however, started well before the George W. Bush Administration in the 1990s.

Donald Gregg, former U.S. ambassador to South Korea under President George H.W. Bush, on June 22, 2005, coauthored an Op-Ed piece with Don Oberdorfer, former *Washington Post* reporter, claiming they had delivered a message from Kim Jong Il to the White House in November 2002, one month after the United States had confronted Pyongyang over the secret uranium enrichment facility it had built in violation of the Agreed Framework and the NPT. Excerpts from the message from Kim read, "If the United States recognizes our sovereignty and assures nonaggression, it is our view that we should be able to find a way to resolve the nuclear issue in compliance with the demands of a new century....If the United States makes a bold decision, we will respond accordingly." Gregg and Oberdorfer urged the Administration to negotiate directly with North Korea.

Thus far, however, Washington has insisted that North Korea come to terms with all five other players with security stakes in this issue—China, Japan, Russia, South Korea and the United States. North Korea's nuclear programs present a regional security challenge, not just a bilateral one. Five rounds of "six-party" multilateral talks with North Korea began in August 2003 in Beijing. The first phase of the fifth round ended November 11, 2005. All five states agree that the Korean peninsula should remain nonnuclear but have disagreed on the right approach for coaxing North Korea into the nonnuclear world.

North Korea wants to secure a bilateral nonaggression pact from Washington, ending the 53-year-old armistice signed at the end of the Korean War, which could also lead to diplomatic recognition. The DPRK also wants substantial economic assistance to bolster its ailing economy and the removal of all U.S. troops from South Korea. If the United States meets these conditions, then North Korea will con-

sider dismantling its nuclear weapons programs in stages. At first, the Bush Administration wanted North Korea to scrap its nuclear weapons programs without conditions. Any new arrangement must include a rigorous on-site inspection and verification system. In return, Washington would pledge not to attack North Korea and relax curbs on economic assistance. American diplomats have reduced their basic demands to four words: "complete, verifiable and irreversible dismantlement."

On June 10, 2005, a full year after the North Koreans had boycotted the six-party talks, President Bush met with South Korean leader Roh Moo-hyun, who has resisted the tougher American approach in favor of more engagement with Pyongyang. The United States said it hoped China and South Korea could convince the North Koreans to come back to the regional talks. South Korea wanted a "softer side of

Sears" and less hammering with hostile rhetoric from the Bush Administration. On June 22, North and South Korean delegations met and pledged to "take real measures for peaceful resolution of the nuclear issue through dialogue," without agreeing to resume the six-party talks. South Korea agreed to provide humanitarian aid to the North, as well as work on joint agriculture ventures. On the same day, in a nod from the Bush Administration to its South Korean ally, the United States announced it would provide 50,000 metric tons of food to North Korea as a "humanitarian gesture" it claimed was unrelated to the nuclear standoff.

On September 19, 2005, after the fourth round of intense negotiations, diplomats released a joint statement that, at least on paper, seemed to solve the problem. North Korea, for its part, "committed to abandoning all nuclear weapons and existing nuclear programs and returning at an early date to the NPT and to IAEA safeguards." The United States, for its part, "affirmed that it has no nuclear weapons on the Korean peninsula and has no intention to attack or invade the DPRK with nuclear or conventional weapons." Each side received key assurances. The Americans got a promise from North Korea to denuclearize, and the North Koreans got their assurance that the United States would not invade and change the North Korean regime. And North Korea also received offers of energy assistance from South Korea for 2 million kilowatts of electric power.

At the fifth round of talks, held from November 9 to 11, 2005, all parties agreed to formulate concrete plans to fulfill the joint statement. Ultimately, the ball remains in North Korea's court. Pyongyang must demonstrate its sustained commitment to transparency, cooperation and internationally verifiable disarmament. By March 2006, however, in response to plans for U.S.-South Korean military exercises in the region, North Korea said it would postpone scheduled high level talks with South Korea, and "strengthen its peaceful nuclear activity." While there may be a joint statement that suggests a North Korean nuclear deal, the devil will be in the details as they play out on the ground, under a watchful international eye.

3

9/11 as Watershed—
Nonproliferation as Continuity

IN HIS BOOK, *Surprise, Security, and the American Experience*, cold-war historian John Lewis Gaddis reflects that unusual surprises and tragic events occasionally link "the historical to the personal." The assassination of President John F. Kennedy on November 22, 1963, proved one such event for one generation; the Japanese attack on Pearl Harbor on December 7, 1941, for another. The Pearl Harbor attack changed the everyday lives of everyone "so that particular December 7th eclipses all the others." According to Gaddis, "September 11, 2001, before the morning had even ended, attained a similar status in our minds. We all remember what we were doing when we heard the news. And we will remember it all over again, when future September 11ths roll around for the rest of our lives."

For the early part of our history, oceans brought us to the new world as well as protected us in large part from foreign invasion. Our heralded American optimism, Gaddis believes, stems in part from not having to worry on a daily basis about our security. "The American ideal—the reason so many people over so many years were willing to risk so much to *become* Americans—had been to insulate domestic life from a violent external world." During the cold war, the danger of nuclear attack never went away, but for many American strategists, "security came to reside…precisely in the fact that the United States and the Soviet Union did have thousands of missiles, armed with nuclear warheads, aimed at one another." That mutual vulnerability provided an ironic sense of security in a world that could incinerate itself many times over.

The 9/11 attacks on New York and Washington brought with them the shock of surprise "at an unexpected time and in an even more unexpected way.…Suddenly Americans could no longer confidently work, travel, or even stay at home without fearing for their lives." This proved a watershed for the American psyche, let alone for its leaders who had to confront and answer this new threat to U.S. security, a set of enemies who did not play fair, who neither played by the rules of deterrence nor made formal declarations of war. In a form of suicidal jujitsu, terrorists used our own planes and manipulated our freedom of travel to attack symbols of our economic and military might—the twin towers and the Pentagon. Al Qaeda also targeted but failed to attack the White House, a key American political symbol.

Gaddis also notes that Americans, when faced with adversity, and particularly surprise attacks, take the offensive "by becoming more conspicuous, by confronting, neutralizing and, if possible, overwhelming the sources of danger rather than fleeing from them." On the flip side, in some circles this can bring with it its own set of picaresque neuroses like building bomb shelters, finding Communists under every rug, or fearing terrorists lurking on every street corner—thus ironically giving in to the very fear that terrorists use as currency to

BALABAN/CARTOONISTS & WRITERS SYNDICATE/cartoonweb.com

undermine the freedoms that Americans hold so dear.

And 9/11 also brought together the fears of nuclear destruction—a cold-war problem—with the fears of a terrorist attack—a post-9/11 problem. The threat of the nexus of WMD and terrorism has driven U.S. policy into a proactive set of strategies aimed at "confronting, neutralizing and, if possible, overwhelming the sources of danger." Proactive, and when necessary, preemptive nonproliferation have taken center stage in a post-9/11 world, with special attention being paid to Iraq, Iran and North Korea. Proactive and particularly preemptive counterterrorism activities have taken precedence in conducting a global war on terrorism.

Equally important, Gaddis concludes, in the course and history of U.S. foreign relations, American leaders tend to think "safety comes from enlarging, rather than contracting, its [the U.S.] sphere of responsibilities." If the original 13 colonies could expand across a continent, no island nation like Britain could rule the United States. The Louisiana Purchase (1803), the Mexican-American (1846–48) and Spanish-American (1898) wars, the Monroe Doctrine (1823), and Manifest Destiny (1845) all spoke to this expansionist theme. When pushing for U.S. entry into World War I, Democratic President Woodrow Wilson argued that America needed "to make the world safe for democracy," a recurrent theme heard repeatedly (and in remarkably similar prose) from the Republican President George W. Bush, today focusing on the need for building democracy in Iraq to improve U.S. security and serve as a beacon for political reform across the Middle East. After Pearl Harbor, Democratic President Roosevelt mobilized the country for war against fascism. After World War II, Presidents Truman and Eisenhower expanded America's global responsibilities to rebuild European and Japanese political and economic stability, while forming NATO and building a global military and nuclear presence, at great cost, designed to deter the threat and expansion of communism. The end of the cold war witnessed the "enlargement" of NATO to Eastern Europe.

Every one of the four nuclear eras since World War II has involved the United States dealing with a dominant threat—the Nazis, the Soviets, the spread of nuclear weapons to other nations, and now, terrorists. While the World War II and cold-war eras have clearly ended, their legacy lives on through the fears generated about dictators and their regimes acquiring nuclear devices, through the remaining nuclear arsenals created during the cold war and afterward, through the perception that nuclear weapons somehow make nations safer or a political cause more just, and the vast amount of nuclear weapons materials now causing mankind so many headaches. The two important follow-on races—against nuclear proliferation to more nations and against the transfer of nuclear weapons to terrorists—derive from the first two races.

September 11, 2001, as a watershed security event, brought with it a continuity of approach that expanded responsibilities at home (the Department of Homeland Security) and abroad (global war on terrorism, with "battles" in Afghanistan and Iraq) to protect America from a new nuclear proliferation threat linked directly to catastrophic terrorism. The fourth nuclear race, a human race against terrorists acquiring nuclear weapons, stems from the realities U.S. and other world leaders chose to face after 9/11. To win this fourth race, the world must simultaneously win the third race against nuclear proliferation that it has fought since the dawn of the nuclear age. This will require strong doses of leadership, patience, international cooperation and creative diligence as humankind strives to confront, neutralize and overwhelm these new sources of danger to civilization. In so doing, nations can collectively help push back the minute hand on that Doomsday Clock now sitting at seven minutes to midnight.

Talking It Over

A Note for Students and Discussion Groups

This issue of the HEADLINE SERIES, like its predecessors, is published for every serious reader, specialized or not, who takes an interest in the subject. Many of our readers will be in classrooms, seminars, or community discussion groups. Particularly with them in mind, we present below some discussion questions—suggested as a starting point only—and references for further reading, as well as pertinent online resources.

Discussion Questions

Americans tend to think about nuclear weapons in two predominant ways: either they represent just another form of weaponry, or they represent a qualitatively different form of weaponry that cannot be considered as just another part of our arsenal. What do you think about nuclear weapons, and why? On what assumptions do you base your opinion? Should the United States build nuclear "bunker busters"?

How has 9/11 changed the ways the United States thinks about nuclear weapons? In what ways do Americans still think the same and in what ways must they think differently? How do you assess the current three-pronged strategy of counterproliferation, nonproliferation and consequence management to combat WMD? If you agree with the strategy, why? If you disagree with it, what do you propose to do differently? How should Washington deal with Iranian and North Korean nuclear weapons aspirations and programs? How should it deal with terrorists who seek nuclear weapons?

Why do nations build nuclear weapons in the first place? Why do terrorists seek the power and the potential destruction they convey? How worried should Americans remain about nuclear terrorism? Why would nations want to share nuclear weapons with terrorists? What about nuclear entrepreneurs? What do the United States, its allies and international organizations do to prevent nuclear smuggling? What lessons can Libya's renunciation of WMD and the discovery of the A.Q. Khan nuclear yard-sale network provide us with for countering smuggling and proliferation? How can Libya serve as a role model for other states?

In each of the four races since the dawn of nuclear proliferation, what prompted the nations involved to build the bomb? Can nuclear proliferation be prevented if a nation decides that "going nuclear" suits its national interests? What resources, including the NPT, should be used to keep proliferation in check? What new measures should be considered? When proliferation happens, what can be done? as a nation? as allies? as an international community?

To what extent should the existing nonproliferation regime be repaired? To what degree should its institutions like the International Atomic Energy Agency be empowered with more authority to inspect for proliferation, destroy nuclear weapons when they find them, and enforce the NPT? To what has the "nuclear bargain" found in the NPT lost traction and served to promote rather than hinder nuclear proliferation?

The end of the cold war and the breakup of the Soviet Union brought new proliferation challenges, and 9/11 brought yet another layer of problems. What are those challenges, and who can best deal with them? To what extent do socioeconomic and demographic challenges lie at the heart of new regional cold wars? Must they be dealt with at the same time that nuclear weapons are dealt with?

What are the pros and cons of marrying counterproliferation and preemption with counterterrorism strategies? What lessons can be learned from 30 years of experience in trying to thwart the Iraqi nuclear weapons programs? What trade-offs do you see in policies that encourage "carrot-and-stick" type approaches? Do you think that the current crises in U.S. relations with Iran and North Korea merit different approaches than before? Do you think that Iran and Iraq want to develop a nuclear stick so they can leverage more negotiated carrots?

Annotated Reading List

Albright, David, and Hinderstein, Corey, "Unraveling the A.Q. Khan and Future Proliferation Networks." *The Washington Quarterly*, Spring 2005. This article describes how A. Q. Khan exploited loopholes in national and international systems to create a secret network that sold nuclear technology to Iran, Libya, North Korea, and perhaps others.

Allison, Graham, *Nuclear Terrorism: The Ultimate Preventable Catastrophe.* New York, Henry Holt & Co., 2005. The founding dean of the John F. Kennedy School of Government and former assistant secretary of defense for policy outlines the threat posed by nuclear terrorism that can be prevented by focusing on a strategy that denies terrorists access to nuclear weapons and nuclear materials.

Bee, Ronald J., "Weapons of Mass Destruction: What Now After 9/11?" *Great Decisions 2004*. New York, Foreign Policy Association, 2004.

Bhatia, Shyam, and McGrory, Daniel, *Brighter than the Baghdad Sun: Saddam Hussein's Nuclear Threat to the United States*. Washington, D.C., Regnery Publishing, 2000. Describes how Saddam invested over $18 billion and employed over 20,000 technicians in his secret nuclear bomb projects, revealed after the Persian Gulf war of 1991. Highly critical of the Clinton-Gore record on Iraq.

Blix, Hans, *Disarming Iraq*. New York, Pantheon Books, 2004. The Swedish former director of the UN inspection commission gives his account of the search for WMD in Iraq that became after the U.S. invasion, in his words, "weapons of mass disappearance."

Bush, George W., *We Will Prevail: President George W. Bush on War, Terrorism, and Freedom*. New York, Continuum International Publishing Group, 2003. A catalogue of President Bush's most significant speeches and addresses on the war on terror, axis of evil, and America's new international policies since 9/11.

Butler, Richard, and Roy, James Charles, *The Greatest Threat: Iraq, Weapons of Mass Destruction, and the Crisis of Global Security*. New York, PublicAffairs, 2001. The Australian ambassador and former chairman of UNSCOM (1992–97) starts his book with a quote from Edmund Burke: "The only thing necessary for the triumph of evil is for good men to do nothing."

Campbell, Kurt M., Einhorn, Robert J., and Reiss, Mitchell B., eds., *The Nuclear Tipping Point: Why States Reconsider Their Nuclear Choices*. Washington, D.C., Brookings Institution Press, 2004. Three former government officials and proliferation experts assemble their and other expert opinions on why states go nuclear and, perhaps more important, why states choose not to go nuclear. They also treat current and future threats.

Cirincione, Joseph, Wolfsthal, Jon B., and Rajkumar, Miriam, *Deadly Arsenals: Nuclear, Biological and Chemical Threats*. Washington, D.C., Carnegie Endowment for International Peace, 2005. A second edition of an excellent study of the major issues surrounding nuclear as well as biological and chemical weapons—including recent developments in Iran, North Korea, Iraq, Libya and nuclear trafficking.

Claire, Rodger W., *Raid on the Sun: Inside Israel's Secret Campaign that Denied Saddam the Bomb*. New York, Random House, 2005. An excellent account of Israel's June 7, 1981, Operation Babylon that draws on interviews with the Israeli pilots who conducted the "preemptive nonproliferation" raid on Saddam's Osirak reactor, thus delaying his efforts to acquire a nuclear weapon.

Cohen, Avner, *Israel and the Bomb*. New York, Columbia University Press, 1999. Among the best books available on the development of Israel's "ambiguous arsenal."

Diehl, Sarah J., and Moltz, James Clay, *Nuclear Weapons and Nonproliferation: A Reference Handbook*. Santa Barbara, Calif., ABC-CLIO, 2002. An excellent compendium of nuclear history and events that includes nuclear documents from World War II through the Bush-Putin Moscow Treaty.

Eberstadt, Nicholas, *End of North Korea*. Washington, D.C., American Enterprise Institute for Public Policy Research,

1999. The AEI-based North Korea expert argues that prolonging North Korea's life may increase the costs and dangers of its inevitable demise.

Gabel, Josiane, "The Role of U.S. Nuclear Weapons After September 11." *The Washington Quarterly*, Winter 2004/2005. An excellent survey by a researcher at the D.C.-based Center for Strategic and International Studies that looks at the literature on what has changed in nuclear weapons policy since 9/11.

Gaddis, John Lewis, *Surprise, Security, and the American Experience*. Cambridge, Mass., Harvard University Press, 2005. A preeminent historian of containment discusses America's response to 9/11, arguing that the new Bush grand strategy of transformation lies in 19th-century traditions of unilateralism, preemption and hegemony, this time on a global scale.

Hartung, William D., "Prevention, Not Intervention: Curbing the New Nuclear Threat." *World Policy Journal*, Winter 2002/2003. The director of the Arms Trade Resource Center argues that "prevention, and not intervention" should dictate American policy toward nuclear weapons, and that Bush's strategy of abandoning the ABM Treaty, plans for nuclear bunker busters and preoccupation with Iraq are mistakes. More diplomatic and multilateral approaches are needed.

Holloway, David, *Stalin and the Bomb: The Soviet Union and Atomic Energy 1939–56*. New Haven, Conn., Yale University Press, 1994. A comprehensive and authoritative study of Stalin's nuclear weapons policies and programs.

McNamara, Robert S., "Apocalypse Soon." *Foreign Policy*, May–June 2005. America's secretary of defense during the Cuban missile crisis contends that the United States must cease relying altogether on nuclear weapons, which remain "immoral, illegal, militarily unnecessary and dreadfully dangerous."

Perkovich, George, *India's Nuclear Bomb: The Impact on Global Proliferation*. Berkeley, University of California Press, 2001. Published soon after India's 1998 nuclear test, an—if not the—authoritative account of India's decision-making about its nuclear weapons program.

Pollack, Kenneth M., *The Persian Puzzle: The Conflict between Iran and America*. New York, Random House, 2005. The former CIA Persian Gulf military analyst and former Clinton NSC director for Persian Gulf affairs, after arguing in an earlier book, *The Threatening Storm*, that the United States needed to invade Iraq, now writes that the United States may need to live with a nuclear Iran.

Sagan, Scott D., and Waltz, Kenneth N., *The Spread of Nuclear Weapons: A Debate Renewed*. New York, W.W. Norton & Co., 2003. Written by two prominent political scientists, the book treats the resumption of a decades-old argument between the two men on the subject of nuclear weapons, with Waltz claiming that proliferation increases international stability, and Sagan arguing that proliferation makes the world significantly more dangerous.

Schwartz, Stephen, ed., *Atomic Audit: The Costs and Consequences of U.S. Nuclear Weapons since 1940*. Washington, D.C., Brookings Institution Press, 1997. The director of a Brookings Institution study details the more than $5 trillion the United States has spent on its nuclear weapons programs.

Wit, Joel S., Gallucci, Robert L., and Poneman, Daniel B., *Going Critical: The First North Korean Nuclear Crisis.* Washington, D.C., Brookings Institution Press, 2005. Three former Clinton officials intimately involved in negotiations that led to the Agreed Framework of 1994 share the lessons learned from those negotiations and offer recommendations on how to apply them to the current nuclear crisis with North Korea.

Online Resources

Arms Control Today: A journal produced by the Arms Control Association, headquartered in Washington, D.C., which tracks the most recent developments in WMD arms control. Every issue lists relevant works, along with recent articles and books on nuclear weapons subjects. Available free online at **www.armscontrol.org/act**

Bunn, Matthew, and Wier, Anthony, *Securing the Bomb 2005: The New Global Imperatives.* Washington, D.C., Project on Managing the Atom, Harvard University and Nuclear Threat Initiative, May 2005. A comprehensive report on the threat of nuclear terrorism, key developments and recommendations, including the appointment of "a senior full-time White House official" to do the heavy lifting needed to focus on this problem. Available free online at **www.nti.org/cnwm**

Bush, George W., *National Strategy to Combat Weapons of Mass Destruction.* Washington D.C., The White House, December 2002. The official government document that spells out its three-pronged strategy for combating all WMD after 9/11: counterproliferation, nonproliferation and consequence management. Available free online at **www.whitehouse. gov/news/releases/2002/12/WMDStrategy.pdf**

Sokolski, Henry, and Clawson, Patrick, eds., *Getting Ready for a Nuclear-Ready Iran*. Strategic Studies Institute, U.S. Army War College, October 2005. The director of the Nonproliferation Policy Education Center and the deputy director of the Washington Institute for Near East Policy have compiled a set of expert essays on the Iranian nuclear threat and the policy options for stopping the Iranian nuclear program. Available free online at **www.strategicstudiesinstitute. army.mil/pubs/display.cfm?PubID=629**

Universal Compliance: A Strategy for Nuclear Security. Washington, D.C., Carnegie Endowment for International Peace, March 2005. A group of nonproliferation experts (George Perkovich, Jessica Tuchman Matthews, Joseph Cirincione, Rose Gottemoeller, Jon Wolfstahl) offers a six-stage blueprint for retooling the international nuclear nonproliferation regime: make nonproliferation irreversible, devalue the currency of nuclear weapons, secure all nuclear materials, stop illegal transfers, undertake conflict resolution, and make Israel, Pakistan and India abide by the NPT. Available free online at **www.carnegieendowment.org/files/UC2.FI-NAL3.pdf**

ARMS CONTROL TODAY **www.armscontrol.org**

THE CARNEGIE ENDOWMENT FOR INTERNATIONAL PEACE
www.ceip.org

THE HENRY L. STIMSON CENTER **www.stimson.org**

MONTEREY INSTITUTE OF INTERNATIONAL STUDIES,
CENTER FOR NONPROLIFERATION STUDIES **www.cns.miis.edu**

NUCLEAR THREAT INITIATIVE **www.nti.org**

COMPLETE THIS FORM AND RETURN TO:
Foreign Policy Association
470 Park Avenue South, 2nd Floor
New York, NY 10016

OR, FAX TO: (212) 481-9275

☐ MR.   ☐ MRS.   ☐ MS.   ☐ DR.   ☐ PROF.

NAME

ADDRESS

APT/FLOOR

CITY _____ STATE _____ ZIP _____

TEL

E-MAIL

☐ AMEX   ☐ VISA   ☐ MC   ☐ CHECK (PAYABLE TO FOREIGN POLICY ASSOCIATION)

CARD NO.

SIGNATURE OF CARDHOLDER   EXP. DATE

I WOULD LIKE TO ORDER	QTY	PRICE
SUBTOTAL	$	
S&H	$	
TOTAL	$	

SHIPPING AND HANDLING:

If order totals	Delivery charge
up to $15.00	$5.00
$15.01–30.00	$6.50
$30.01–60.00	$8.00
$60.01–90.00	$10.50
$90.01–120.00	$12.00
$120.01–150.00	$14.50
$150.01 and over	add 10% of subtotal

HIGHER RATES APPLY TO EXPEDITE SERVICE

↑ Prepayment must accompany all orders from individuals, and must include shipping and handling charges. Libraries, universities and schools using purchase orders may be billed. Contact a customer service representative for more info: 800 477-5836.

↑ All orders outside the U.S. and its possessions must be prepaid. Checks must be in U.S. funds drawn on a U.S. correspondent bank. Please add 35% of subtotal for shipping and handling charges.